coolcamping

cookbook

SECOND EDITION

Tom Tuke-Hastings, Nadia Shireen, Shellani Gupta,
Jonathan Knight, Sophie Dawson & Harriet Yeomans

The publishers assert their right to use
Cool Camping as a trademark of Punk Publishing Ltd.

Cool Camping Cookbook (2nd edition)
This edition published in the United Kingdom in 2012 by
Punk Publishing Ltd
3 The Yard
Pegasus Place
London SE11 5SD

www.punkpublishing.co.uk
www.coolcamping.co.uk

A catalogue record of this book is available from the British Library.

ISBN 978-1-906889-51-7
(ISBN 978-0-9552036-4-0 1st edition)

10 9 8 7 6 5 4 3 2

introduction

Hello. Welcome to the second edition of the *Cool Camping Cookbook*.

We like to think there's something a bit special about cooking and eating in the great outdoors. Licking an ice cream while ambling along the beach, devouring salty fish and chips on a park bench, sinking your teeth into a burger in the back garden, sitting by the campfire toasting marshmallows – it's all good. There's just something about the air, the smells, the sizzles and the earth beneath our feet that makes everything taste better.

The Cool Camping team have been trying out a few more alfresco recipes since the last edition, and we even asked you to send in some of your faves. And this is the result – a little book bursting with over 80 delicious dishes for your outdoor dining pleasure. Cooking in the elements can be as straightforward or as complicated as you like, but we're simple, honest folk, so you'll find most of the recipes here extremely do-able. It's not about creating Michelin-star-rated grub or presenting perfect, airbrushed photos. We don't mind the odd mucky thumbprint on our sandwich or a little bit of grit in our stew – real life is muddy, and all the better for it.

The chapters are vaguely split into how you'll be cooking; with just one pot, on a barbecue or on a campfire. But there's also food for your mood, with sections on 'comfort food' and 'something fancy'. Many of the recipes are interchangeable, anyway, which makes the whole chapter thing a bit unnecessary, but we had to break it up somehow!

The best approach is to flick through until you find something you like the look of. Then get out of the kitchen, into the great outdoors and and give it a go.

Over to you then, campers...

preparation

It's an annoying word, we know. But preparation can mean the difference between tucking into a steaming hot plate of loveliness or gnawing helplessly on a carton of powdered milk. Some of our recipes would benefit from some prep at home, so set a little time aside before your trip if you can.

It's useful to have a rough idea of what you'll be cooking and to prepare and pack what you need. Making a few sauces at home (see p20) and spooning them into tubs or jars is also a sensible precaution, unless you plan on taking a food processor with you. If you don't make your sauces beforehand, pack a potato masher, which does the job of a food processor but is more satisfying!

Before we begin, a few useful things we have learned and would like to share with you:

- Sealable food bags are your friends.
- Don't forget to label food bags with contents, measurements, cooking instructions etc.
- Frozen meat and homemade meals are also your friends. As they defrost, they'll keep your coolbox temperature down.
- Herbs, spices and stock cubes transform your food – dispense as much as you need into food bags (yes, them again).
- Foodstuffs like tinned tomatoes also come in cartons, so ditch the tins to save weight.
- Pitta breads are basically flat-packed food. We love them.
- Some tasty treats prepared at home (p171, p172, p174) and shared around the campfire will always make you popular.
- While self-sufficiency is all well and good, nearby farm shops, ice cream vans and village pubs are not to be sniffed at. Buy local and cut the food miles.

the kit

Deciding how much equipment to take with you on a camping trip is a pretty personal thing. There are those who prefer to sustain themselves armed only with a sharp knife and a packet of matches, while others will think nothing of loading up a four-by-four with a crate of champagne and an impressive selection of mustards.

Whichever camp you fall into, you'll probably find this little checklist quite useful. Photocopy it or download it from www.coolcamping.co.uk and add anything else you think you might need to it. If the worst happens and you forget something – well, then you'll remember for next time. And if you find that taking an ice cream maker along wasn't really necessary, you'll be inclined to leave it at home for your next trip. Chop and change your checklist as you go – with practice comes confidence, comes expertise. Or something.

A handy checklist

Gas, petrol or gel stove

Barbecue

Campfire grill/wire rack

Charcoal

Firewood

Fire starters or newspaper

Pots and pans (don't forget lids)

Cooking utensils

Tongs

Skewers

A very sharp knife

Foil

Tin opener

Bottle opener/corkscrew

Plastic mixing bowls

Mugs/cups

Plates

Cutlery

Oven gloves

Lighter and (waterproof) matches

Potato peeler

Potato masher

Pestle and mortar

Chopping board

Washing-up liquid and brush/sponges

Tea towels

Bin bags

Plastic food bags

Coolbox

Thermos flasks

Weighing scales, if you're fussy about quantities

1 2
3 4

what to cook with

Camping stove

Most campers make do with a trusty old stove (1), and it's amazing what you can get these little things to do – see our one-pot wonder chapter (p26) for inspiration. For longer trips, or if you go camping quite a bit, it's worth investing in a double-hobber, preferably one with a grill underneath (p189). And don't forget the gas refills.

Barbecue

In moments of weakness, it can be tempting to opt for a disposable barbecue from the supermarket or garden centre. These are vaguely acceptable if you're cooking something quick like fish, but they don't give out much heat or last very long. A better option is to use a portable barbecue – both gas and charcoal ones are readily available. But for maximum brownie points, build your own simple barbecue (2) with a bed of coals, and a few bricks or logs either side to support a grill. Somehow, food tastes better on a barbie you've built yourself. See p51 for more barbecue tips.

Campfire

The original and still the best way to cook, no question, but campfire cooking does require a little effort. You'll need kindling to get the fire going and a good supply of logs to feed it. Invest in some of Light My Fire's equipment (see p188), designed by professional fire-starters. Cook over the flames with a big cast-iron cooking pot, also known as a Dutch oven (3), or by plonking a special skillet thing (p189) over the top. Alternatively, wait until the fire has died down and cook directly on the coals, or place a grill over the heat to use as a barbecue. You can also pierce things on sticks and hold them over the flames; a timeless and sociable way to cook. See p75 for more on campfires.

Other stuff

We're big fans of the Cobb Grill (4), a portable little thing that can be used for roasting, baking, frying and smoking as well as barbecuing. It's highly efficient, environmentally friendly and cooks everything to perfection. We also mentioned a Dutch oven above, which we use as a campfire cooking pot. This becomes a whole new toy when used in the 'proper' way – by placing around 20 hot coals on the lid and another 10 under the pot. This cooks everything evenly and opens up the possibility of baking at camp. For stockists, see p188.

foraging

Because we are but a swarm of ants on the surface of Mother Nature's picnic blanket, here are a few words on enjoying the fruits of our abundant countryside (while avoiding any nasty stuff that could leave us blue and stiff with our legs in the air).

So what to pick? Well, in springtime, young nettle tops, wild garlic leaves and other spring shoots are a welcome addition to salads and frying pans. The summer months bring with them delicate elderflower leaves, and in late July and August there are all sorts of sweet, juicy berries to squish between your fingers. Wild mushrooms flourish in the autumn, bringing weird and wonderful smells to the cooking pot.

Seasonal and regional variations will determine what you find on your investigative rambles. So before setting off, take the time to do a little research and work out which particular local delicacies you'll be searching for.

Some important things to remember:

- Carry a reliable, well-illustrated plant and fungi guide; many plants have edible bits and toxic bits. Make sure your book tells you which is which. And if you're not sure, then don't pick it.
- Sturdy gloves will protect your hands from nettles and thorns. And sticks are handy for pushing aside brambles and yanking down overhead branches.
- Hedgerows by busy roads or old industrial sites aren't spots you want to pick food from.
- Don't be greedy – only pick as much as you need.
- Don't let dogs go foraging on their own.
- Don't disturb sleepy woodland creatures, birds' nests, caterpillars, worms, beetles or any other living things.
- Keep a little piece of your foraged plant or mushroom aside, so that if the worst happens and someone has a reaction, the culprit can be identified.
- Uprooting a wild plant without permission from a landowner is illegal. For more information, visit the Food Standards Agency website (www.food.gov.uk).

Good places to go for more
information about foraging:
The Forestry Commission: www.forestry.gov.uk
The Woodland Trust: www.woodlandtrust.org.uk
The Association of British Fungus Groups: www.abfg.org
The British Mycological Society: www.britmycolsoc.org.uk
A man called Fergus, who's an expert forager: www.wildmanwildfood.co.uk

a note on behalf of Mother Earth

Warning: hippy alert.

It's simple really. The good, green Earth has been kind enough to give us all sorts of lovely things to enjoy, like trees, hills, squawky birds, sea, sand and sunshine.

And in return, all it asks of us is that we take a little care of our surroundings. So keep it green, people.

- Leave every site just as you found it.
- Don't wash dirty pans and plates in running water – instead, wipe them first with a biodegradable detergent, and then with a damp cloth.
- Take every last bit of rubbish with you – this includes bottle tops, tin lids, scrappy bits of foil, cigarette butts and dead matches.
- Pop any leftover food in a bin bag to throw away later – don't just sling it on the grass. Hedgehogs probably shouldn't be eating ratatouille.
- If you find an ecological wonder like a nest, warren or den, by all means point and stare at it, but do not touch, poke or in any way harass it.
- Don't carve your initials into an unsuspecting tree. Give it a hug instead.

a vegan's guide

Dixe Wills is the author of *Tiny Campsites* and co-author of *Cool Camping* guides, a non-flying travel writer for the *Guardian* and someone who generally spends an awful lot of time in the great outdoors. He also happens to exist on an entirely vegan diet – and it doesn't seem to have done him any harm. Well, see for yourselves… here he is chatting about the benefits of going vegan on your camping trip.

Vegan food and camping. Now, if you're not already a vegan, you might be labouring under the misapprehension that the two are not a match made in heaven.

Labour no more. Nowadays, you'll be relieved to learn, vegan cuisine is not all organic gravel served in parboiled sea water. Indeed, experts from many nations agree that some of the best oh-no-I've-only-got-one-stove-and-a-couple-of-tiny-pots recipes involve no meat or dairy products, both of which can be difficult to bring along camping anyway if you don't have access to a fridge to keep them chilled and fresh.

There are also the budgetary benefits of vegan eating to consider. Doing away with expensive fish, meat and even cheese on your camping shopping list will have you smugly patting your back pocket as you reach the till.

And let's not even get started on the health benefits and the number of times you'll be able to hit your 'five-a-day' quota…

So, treat the vegan recipes featured in this book as mere portals into a delicious world – nay, planet – of gastronomic delights, where the innovative and creative use of vegetables, pulses, spices, herbs, fungi and dairy-free cheese-style slices (also available as a powder) is positively encouraged.

Then, when you leave your campsite in the morning full of, say, scrummy vegan pancakes (p82), you'll find yourself bursting with a previously unknown kinship with farm animals. Cattle, pigs, sheep, chickens and other creatures will look you in the eye and seem to smile. Do they know you won't be eating them or their by-products come lunchtime? I think they do.

dixewills.com

super-quick sauces

Cooking in the outdoors is all about getting the maximum flavour from your food with minimal effort. These tasty sauces can be knocked up in a flash and are extremely versatile – use them as dips, marinades or pour-over sauces. If you're feeling organised you could make them at home and bring them in a jar, but where's the fun in that? Master just a few of these sauces and you'll find cooking at camp an absolute breeze.

olive tapenade

ingredients

1 tbsp of capers, chopped
125g of black or green olives, chopped
3 anchovy fillets, chopped
1 garlic clove, peeled & crushed
1 lemon (juice only)
1–2 tbsp of olive oil
Salt & pepper to taste

method

Mush all the ingredients together using a pestle and mortar until you get a smooth paste. Season as required.

ideal for

Bruschetta (p119) with a difference
Adding to barbecued fish or chicken

lemon and garlic mayo

ingredients

150ml of good-quality mayonnaise
1 lemon (juice only)
1 garlic clove, peeled & crushed

method

Mix all the ingredients together and keep cool. Like the Fonz.

ideal for

Any seafood dish (p54, p63, p136 & p139)
Corn on the cob
Or use it for dipping in chips from the local chippy.

pesto

ingredients

1 garlic clove, peeled & crushed
A handful of fresh basil leaves,
   finely chopped
A handful of parmesan cheese, grated
2 tbsp of olive oil
A handful of pine nuts
A sprinkle of freshly ground black pepper

method

Pound the garlic and basil together using a pestle and mortar. If you don't have a pestle and mortar you can make do with a potato masher. Add the grated parmesan cheese, a glug of olive oil and the pine nuts and mix to a smooth consistency. Season with freshly ground black pepper.

ideal for

Bruschetta (p119)
Bags of salmon (p63)
Extra calzone filling (p89)
Barbecued chicken fillets – slashed diagonally with the pesto sauce smeared all over, wrapped in foil and placed on the barbecue.
Or, if you are stuck, add to a saucepan of cooked pasta and top with cheese.

jerked honey rum glaze

ingredients

1 tsp of jerk seasoning
4 tbsp of runny honey
2 tsp of dark rum

method

Rum may not be your bottle of choice to take along camping, but not only does it make an essential ingredient in this glorious glaze, it'll keep you warm on those cold nights, too. Simply slosh everything together in a nice pot and use as a marinade or brush on meat before and during grilling.

ideal for

Jerk rum ribs (p69), and any other meat going onto the barbecue.

barbecue sauce-o-rama

ingredients

1 garlic clove, whole
3 tbsp of soy sauce
3 tbsp of orange juice
3 tbsp of tomato ketchup
3 tbsp of white wine vinegar
3 tbsp of runny honey
Optional: a dash of something spicy –
Worcester sauce, or tabasco, or a sprinkle of chilli powder/flakes

method

Splosh all the ingredients into a saucepan, in no particular order, and cook up until the sauce thickens.

ideal for

Use as a marinade for meat going on the barbecue (especially ribs), or as dunking sauce, hot or cold. It also goes a treat drizzled over caramelised onions in a hot dog.

minty raita

ingredients

1 small carton of natural yogurt
2 tbsp of mint sauce
1 tsp of turmeric
1 tsp of garam masala
1 tsp of chilli powder
1 tsp of salt

method

Pour the yogurt into a bowl, add the mint sauce and give it a stir. Then add in the spices and salt and mix thoroughly.

ideal for

Lamb chops with couscous (p149)
Spicy lamb koftas (p73)
Paneer and vegetable kebabs (p155)
Dip for any barbecued meat or fish.
Or this makes a nice snacky dip with crisps or crudités.

mango salsa

ingredients

1 ripe mango, peeled, stoned and diced
1 lime (juice only)
1 fresh red chilli, deseeded & diced
2 spring onions, finely chopped
A handful of fresh coriander, chopped

method

Mix all the ingredients together and serve with seafood (p54, p63, p136 & p139) or fishcakes (p39).

Thai green curry paste

ingredients

A bunch of spring onions, chopped into 3–4 pieces
1 fresh bird's-eye chilli, deseeded
A thumb of fresh root ginger, peeled
1 stem of lemon grass, outer leaves removed, chopped into 3–4 pieces
A big handful of fresh basil
2 big handfuls of fresh coriander
1 lime (zest & juice)
A big slug of olive oil
A pinch of sea salt & pepper

method

Ideally, you'll make this one at home and take with you – just whack everything in the food processor and press the button. Once it's smooth and pastey, spoon into a plastic food bag and keep cool until you're ready to use it. If you're making this at camp, chop everything up as small as possible and mush together with a pestle and mortar or potato masher.

ideal for

Fireside fishcakes (p39) and Thai green curry (p95).

beer marinade

ingredients

½ onion, diced
½ green pepper, diced
½ red pepper, diced
½ yellow pepper, diced
½ cucumber, peeled & diced
2 tbsp of olive oil
10 tbsp of beer
Salt & pepper

method

Mix all the ingredients together in a bowl.
Er, that's it.

ideal for

Chicken or pork; use as a marinade,
then barbecue the meat in foil.
Or serve as a dipping sauce with
barbecued chicken or pork.

tip-top guacamole

ingredients

2 squishy avocados (they must be super-
  ripe, or it won't work)
A handful of cherry tomatoes, chopped
1 small red onion, finely chopped
1 fresh red chilli, deseeded & chopped
  (or chilli flakes)
A handful of fresh coriander, chopped
A big old glug of olive oil
Salt & pepper
½ lime (juice only)

method

Mash up the avocados with a fork (or,
even better, with a pestle if you have a
pestle and mortar as part of your kit). Stir
in the tomatoes, onion, chilli and coriander
and continue to mash and grind. Add the
oil, then salt, pepper and lime juice to taste
and mix thoroughly.

ideal for

Skillet fajitas (p80)
Or as a fab chunky dip for tortilla chips
(we heart the lime-flavoured ones).

one-pot wonders

Hardcore campers compete to reduce their kit to the bare minimum, using titanium spoons and cutting off cup handles to save a few grams. But having a very basic kit doesn't mean you need to survive on mud and will-power alone. Try some of these frill-free recipes that'll give you bags of flavour from a little rucksack.

porridge

Porridge is brilliant fuel for the wood-burner of your soul – bung in all sorts of tasty things to liven it up and you'll have enough energy to climb a tree and throw coconuts at your friend's head all day long.

Serves 1–2

ingredients
1 cup of oatmeal
2 cups of water
1 cup of milk
Raisins
Toasted almonds

optional extras
1 banana, peeled and sliced
A fat trickle of maple syrup or honey
Brown sugar
Blackberries, blueberries, raspberries, strawberries

method
Mix the oatmeal, water and milk together and bring to the boil. Simmer and stir – as it starts to thicken, add the raisins and almonds. Turn the heat off once the porridge has thickened. Sprinkle over one of our toppings, if you like, from the list of optional extras, and enjoy while it's steaming hot.

mermaid omelette

Omelettes are the ultimate in fast food. They're quick, easy, tasty and full of eggy goodness. Best of all, you can plonk whatever you like in them, so your ingredients list can vary quite a lot. Well, apart from the eggs bit; they're pretty crucial. This recipe is quite over the top, but will impress even the most jaded omelette gourmet.

Serves 1

ingredients

2 eggs
50g of smoked salmon
A handful of strawberries
1 tbsp of chopped fresh parsley or basil
Salt & pepper
1 tbsp of olive oil

method

Crack the eggs into a large mug or bowl and whisk with a fork. Slice the salmon, quarter the strawberries and add them to the egg mix. Add the parsley or basil, a good grind of salt and pepper, and give everything a stir.

Heat the oil in a frying pan and, when it's nice and hot, pour in the mixture. Once the bottom solidifies, tilt the pan around to expose the runny mixture to the heat.

Wait until the omelette loosens from the bottom, then fold it in half and serve. Eat piping hot, with a glass of Bucks Fizz if you're feeling fancy.

camperstrone

This is just the kind of cockle-warming one-pot wonder you'll be wanting to dish out and yum up when the sun's gone down for the day and you've popped on your hoodie and favourite woolly hat.

Another simple yet delicious dish, Camperstrone has been brought to us by Jill from Happy Camper Holidays. Thanks Jill!

Serves 4–6

ingredients

200g of chorizo sausage, chopped into chunks
300ml of any tomatoey pasta sauce (we like a spicy one)
1 tin of chickpeas (or any other type of bean)
750ml of chicken stock
500g of chunky dried pasta
A big hunk of crusty bread
Grated cheese (optional)
A sprinkling of roughly torn parsley to garnish

method

In a large pan, fry the chorizo until the fat runs and the chunks start to crisp up a little. Drain off a little fat then add the pasta sauce, chickpeas, stock and pasta. Bring to the boil, then reduce the heat and simmer for 12–15 minutes, stirring occasionally and adding a little extra water, if necessary, until the pasta is cooked to your liking.

Serve with crusty bread, and maybe some grated cheese, with a little parsley to garnish.

> **veggies**
> omit the chorizo, add an extra can of a different bean variety of your choice, use vegetable stock, and serve with a generous handful of cheese.

ramen noodle soup

This stuff is hot, filling and delicious; the chilli gives it a kick that warms you up from the inside. And it's a one-pot dish, so there's less washing-up. Bonus.

Serves 1

ingredients

1 steak fillet
1 beef stock cube (or chicken stock, for a lighter flavour)
1cm of fresh ginger
1 fresh red chilli
1 cake of dried noodles
3 spring onions
A small handful of mangetout
A small handful of beansprouts
1 lime (juice only)
A small handful of fresh coriander
Salt & pepper

method

Cook the steak over a hot heat for a short while so that it is well browned on each side, then put aside and allow to cool. Boil just over half a pot of water (less if you have a large pot) and add the stock cube.

Peel and dice the ginger finely, deseed and thinly slice the chilli and add both to the boiling water with the noodles. Stir the noodles to help break them up.

Slice the spring onions and add them to the soup. When the noodles are nearly cooked, add the mangetout and beansprouts. Bring to the boil, then turn off the heat. Slice up or shred the steak and then mix it into the soup with the lime juice and some chopped coriander. Taste and season to your liking.

Serve from the pot or in a bowl with some extra slices of steak on top and a little sprinkle of extra coriander. Be sure to slurp up the broth as well as chomping on the noodles.

Dave Richards originally created his Barefoot Chef (thebarefootchef.com) persona for a photography project, which went on to spawn a number of comedy cookery videos on YouTube. Since then his alter ego has developed a life of its own and has a column in *VW Camper* magazine. He was also a regular cookery contributor on a radio show until he made the crew a tasty squirrel stew and was never invited back...

Barefoot Chef's Moroccan chicken

This recipe started life as a complicated multi-pan job, but Dave Richards, the Barefoot Chef, has gradually honed it down the barefoot way and, astonishingly, it looks and tastes essentially the same as it did when it took hours to prepare and had hundreds of ingredients. See for yourselves.

Serves 4

ingredients

400g of chicken fillets
2 onions
1–2 garlic cloves, peeled
1 tsp of paprika
100g of ripe apricots
75g of basmati rice
A handful of black olives

A splash of vegetable oil
1 tin of chopped tomatoes
1 tin of chickpeas, drained
125ml of boiling water
2 tbsp of honey
Salt & pepper

method

Start by boiling the kettle and dicing the chicken.

Then set about chopping the onions, garlic and apricots and preparing the amounts of paprika, rice and olives. Better still – prepare them at home and pack them into one big container to take with you, so they're all ready for the pot.

Now for the easy bit: heat the oil in a large pan, add the chicken and then all the other ingredients. Give it a bit of a stir and then bring to the boil, cover the saucepan and let the delicious ricey-stewy concoction simmer for about 40 minutes.

Th-th-th-that's all folks! You're free to scoff the lot. Why not wash it all down with an authentic mug of Moroccan mint tea? If you're lucky enough to be camping by a river, just pick some delicious fresh river mint and pop three large leaves into a mug of hot water with sugar to taste. Souk-tastic!

fireside fishcakes

Fishcakes can be packed with flavour and are simple to make. It's easier to prepare the mix at home and squish them into shape when you're ready to cook, but you can also make these at camp if you have a potato masher. Thai green curry paste will give these an exotic zing and save you having to seek out fresh lemon grass in the rural wilderness.

Serves 2

ingredients

A 250g salmon fillet (skinless)
1 large or 2 small boiled potatoes
3 tbsp of Thai green curry paste
  (see p23 if you want to make your own)
1 spring onion
A handful of fresh coriander

Salt & pepper
1 egg yolk
1 lime (juice only)
Breadcrumbs
2 tbsp of vegetable oil
Limes, rice and mango salsa (p23), to serve

method

Roughly chop the fish and potatoes and blitz in a food processor (or squash with a potato masher) until it reaches a smooth consistency. Stir in the curry paste. Slice the spring onion, chop the coriander and mix together with a little salt, pepper and the egg yolk. If it looks too dry, squeeze in a bit of lime juice. Sling the whole lot in a food bag and keep cool until cooking time.

When you're ready to cook, divvy up the mixture and roll it into golf-ball shapes. Coat the balls with breadcrumbs and squish them into patties. Gently fry them on each side in a little oil for a few minutes – don't hassle them too much or they may break apart. When they're cooked through, squeeze over with lime wedges and serve with hot rice and a good dollop of mango salsa.

---

important fishcake information

If you're making the mixture beforehand, note that it should be kept as cool as possible, preferably refrigerated. You could always freeze the mix to keep it cooler for longer, if you wanted to be clever about it.

Mrs Gupta's potato curry

Mrs Gupta, mother-in-law of our chief camper at Tent HQ, has been cooking this tasty little curry dish since her childhood in Ludhiana, northern India, and she bought it with her to Hitchin, Hertfordshire, in 1971. She has cooked it more than 1,000 times, but has never measured out the exact quantities or written down the recipe – until now.

Please note, quantities may be wildly inaccurate – but that's the joy of curries; increase/decrease spice amounts according to your taste.

Serves 2

ingredients

A glug of vegetable oil
Around 1 tsp of ground cumin
1 white onion, diced (maybe 2 if
  they're small)
About 2cm of fresh ginger, finely chopped
Maybe 4 garlic cloves, peeled & crushed
1 tin of chopped tomatoes
1 tbsp of turmeric
1 tbsp of garam masala
About ½ tbsp of red chilli powder

1 tbsp of tomato purée
A pinch of salt
2–3 large spuds (King Edward or Desirée
  make for a good texture, but any will do)
125ml of water
1 lime (juice only)
1 tbsp of sugar
A handful of fresh coriander, finely
  chopped, to garnish
Rice or naan, to serve

method

Warm some oil in the saucepan, add the cumin, onion, ginger and garlic, and stir until brown. Add the tin of chopped tomotoes, mix together then add the turmeric, garam masala, chilli powder and tomato purée. Sprinkle some salt on top, then stir for 2 minutes over a low heat.

Peel the potatoes and chop into small cubes. Add them to the pan along with the water, a squeeze of fresh lime juice and the sugar, then bring to the boil and simmer for around 20–25 minutes or until the spuds have softened and the sauce has thickened. Sprinkle some coriander on top and serve with rice or naan.

This also makes a great camping breakfast, served with toast.

caring, sharing soup fondue

Festivals. Parties. Football. Sex. Some things just get better when more people are involved. This is a really communal, let's-all-huddle-around-the-campfire kind of recipe. Rather than the traditional cheese or oil fondues, you use stock as your cooking fluid, dunk in all sorts of savoury treats, and then drink up the broth.

Serves 4

ingredients
Various vegetables to dunk: try courgettes, broccoli, pre-cooked potatoes, asparagus
4 chicken breasts
1 lemon (juice only)
Salt & pepper
2 litres of chicken stock
1 onion, quartered

method
Cut the vegetables into bite-size pieces and arrange them on a plate.

Slice the chicken breasts up thinly, squeeze over the juice of a lemon and grind on some salt and freshly ground black pepper.

Put the stock in a big pan, add the onion and chicken breast pieces, bring to the boil and simmer for 10 minutes. Now let everyone spear veggies from the plate and dip into the stock to cook. You might want to use a few extra fondue forks so you can have couple of things on the go at the same time. Try not to fight over snagging the tasty chunks of chicken that should be floating about in the broth. When all the veggies and chicken have been scoffed, drink the hot soup, which should have absorbed the added flavours. Some crusty, buttered bread would top it off a treat. Anyone for a round of 'Kumbaya'?

> **top tip**
> If you don't have fondue forks, cut the bark off some sticks, sharpen them up and then get jabbing to your heart's content.

Napom's chunky hash

Corned beef. A staple cupboard-content of many a 1950s household that was first mass-produced during the Industrial Revolution. Tins of this salt-preserved stuff still command a spot on supermarket shelves and last a good long time, so are just the job for your camping larder.

Napom (short for Helen, who's a member of the Pom family and a keen camper) concocted this corned beef-based dish as an easy meal to cook at any time of day, but she thinks it makes the best brekkie, and we're inclined to agree.

Serves 4

ingredients

Sunflower oil
5 leftover or boiled potatoes (best with
 skins on), chopped into chunks
1 onion, chopped
1 tin of corned beef
400g of baked beans
Chilli ketchup

Tabasco sauce (Worcester sauce works
 well, if you prefer)
4 eggs
Salt & pepper
Some good bread for mopping up
 eggy, beany juices

method

Heat a glug of oil in a large pan and fry the potato pieces and chopped onion until brown and crispy.

Break the corned beef into chunks and add to the pan with the baked beans and sauces of your choice to taste – chilli ketchup works particularly well and is great if you're in need of a wake-me-up kick!

Cook the mix for as long as you like – crispy is good, but try to keep the texture chunky. In the meantime fry the eggs (in the same pan if you have room).

Season before serving with fresh bread and a steaming brew.

ratatouille

And lo, it was deemed that along with crisp sandwiches and vodka jelly, every student in the known universe would subsist on ratatouille until the end of term time. But this humble dish can actually be hugely satisfying, as long as it's left to burble away on a low heat for a decent amount of time. Maybe play a game of charades while you wait.

Serves 2

ingredients

1 red onion
1 tbsp of olive oil
1 red pepper
Salt & pepper
A couple of garlic cloves, peeled
1 tbsp of Herbes de Provence
Some fresh, local veggies, chopped
1 tin of chopped tomatoes
A glass of red wine
2 tbsp of tomato purée
Fresh herbs
Fresh, dunkable bread with butter

method

Slice the onion and soften in some olive oil in a pan. While this is cooking, slice the pepper and add to the pan with a little salt and pepper. Squish the garlic cloves and add to the pan, along with the Herbes de Provence. Now would also be a good time to add any extra vegetables – courgettes and carrots both work well.

When everything starts softening nicely, chuck in the tomatoes. Add a heavy-handed glug of red wine and the tomato purée. Bring the whole lot to the boil, then turn the heat down and allow it to cook for at least 30 minutes, stirring occasionally. Season with further salt and pepper to taste and any fresh herbs you have lying around.

Dunk in comforting wodges of buttered bread and eat while piping hot.

four-can stew

Officially the easiest meal in the world? Only if you have a tin-can opener, otherwise it's probably the toughest…

Helen invented this recipe when she was stuck for something quick and wholesome to cook for supper. It became a fast family fave and no wonder – it's four-can tasty!

Serves 4

ingredients

1 tbsp of olive oil
1 onion, chopped
4 garlic cloves, peeled & crushed
3 tins of differing beans of your choice –
 kidney, black-eyed & borlotti, perhaps

1 tin of chopped tomatoes
1 sachet of taco seasoning mix
A bag of tortilla chips
Good bread or sautéed potatoes
Grated cheese

method

Heat the oil in a pan and add the onion and garlic – frying them until they go soft – then add all the beans (minus their liquid, but don't chuck it, you might need some later), the chopped tomatoes and the seasoning mix. Give the mixture a good stir before popping a lid over the pan and letting it stew for about 20–30 minutes, adding the leftover bean liquid if necessary.

Stir the stew before serving either in big bowls with the tortilla chips crushed on top along with a side of bread or potatoes, or in a giant dish on top of a layer of tortilla chips with grated cheese on the top for a sharing platter of nacho love.

---

note for meat-eaters
Feel free to add sausages to the stew – pork and chilli ones work especially well.

the barbecue bible

There's nothing quite like the sizzling sound of a well-oiled steak on a hot barbecue grill to drive otherwise reasonable human beings into salivating, primal meat-monsters. Grr. Arrg. Grr.

tips for successful barbecuing...

- Don't pitch your barbecue in a windy spot. Avoid being too near fences, trees, plants or buildings.
- You need to pitch on solid, even ground – the whole contraption must be stable.
- New barbecue? Let it burn off for a good 10 minutes, and wipe the grill with a little oil. This should stop food from sticking to the surface.
- Making your own barbecue? Use rocks, bricks or damp logs to mark out the area and contain the coals. Bricks can be used to alter the height of your grill, as the heat from the coals will vary.
- Make sure all the food you want to cook is vaguely the same thickness, so it all cooks through at the same rate.
- Keep any excitable children and pets well away.
- Keep a bucket of water or a fireblanket nearby, just in case.

- Don't let drunk people cook.
- Don't use liquid paraffin or alcohol to get the flames going.
- Special paraffin-free barbecue firelighters are available that won't make your food smell and taste horrible.
- Wait until the flames have died down and the coals are white before you start cooking.
- A good way to check if it's ready is to hold your hand over the heat. If you can keep it there for 4 or 5 seconds, it's ready to cook. Any less, it's still too hot.
- If necessary, spread the coals around a bit before cooking to give an even heat.
- Once cooking, keep an eye out for hotter and cooler parts of the barbie and shift your food around accordingly.
- A scattering of dried herbs over the coals makes everything smell amazing.

barbecue-starting for dummies

If you're one of those people who can't get a barbie going with firelighters, try this method. Scrunch up a few sheets of newspaper, pile them together and build a tipi of kindling over it. Light the paper, wait for the kindling to catch, then quickly add more kindling to feed the flames, leaving space between and underneath the wood for the air to circulate freely. Gradually start adding charcoal to the top – the trick is not to smother the flames but to let them burn through the coals. If the charcoal doesn't catch this time, no offence, like, but you probably shouldn't be the person in charge of the barbie.

the gut-buster brekkie

A cup of coffee and an argument with the bus driver may be a typical way to breakfast for most urbanites, but it really is the most important meal of the day when you've just peeled yourself out of a sleeping bag and feel a bit cold and stiff.

This simple fry-up becomes a breakfast of champions if you can get hold of organic bangers and bacon, not to mention fresh farm eggs, with wispy feathers still attached.

Serves 2

ingredients

4 top-quality sausages
1 tin of baked beans
6 cherry tomatoes
2 tsp of oil or butter

Salt & pepper
6 rashers of top-quality bacon
2 fresh farm eggs
Bread

method

Get the fire going and a cuppa in your hand as soon as possible. The key to a great breakfast is patience, so nibble on a hunk of bread with butter to keep you going.

Six items will be competing for space over your heat, so bear that in mind – makeshift foil trays really come into their own here.

Sausages go on first; cook them over a low to moderate heat till they're gooey and juicy.

Beans go on next. They also need a slow cook, so find a cooler spot towards the edge of the barbecue to perch the beanpot.

Coat the cherry tomatoes in a little oil, salt and pepper and place carefully on the grill.

After the sausages have had a good 10–15-minute head start, nudge them to one side so there's enough room to add the bacon.

Make little containers out of a double thickness of foil and pop a little oil or butter in each. When the fat gets hot, crack an egg into each and leave to cook on an idling heat.

Tear up the bread, toast it and smother it in butter. As soon as the eggs are ready, pile everything onto plates, add any seasoning or condiments you fancy and devour.

catch of the day

So simple, but so satisfying – catching your own guarantees a succulent, fresh fish that will need little dressing or accompaniment. Pure, earthy – almost spiritual – this is the holiest of barbecue feasts.

Serves 1

ingredients
Some stonkingly fresh fish
1 lemon (juice only)
Olive oil or butter
Fresh herbs (some thyme or a few bay leaves would be ideal)

method
Catch, gut and clean your fish. You could fry your fish in a pan with a touch of butter, but it's also tempting to lay it directly on the barbecue bars.

Once the bottom side has browned nicely, flip it over. You want the skin to crisp up and blacken with charcoal lines. Have a peek at the flesh – when ready, it should be firm and no longer opalescent.

Eat straight away while piping hot. Although a scattering of fresh herbs would be welcomed here, they are by no means essential. Fresh lemon juice and a drizzle of olive oil or butter will give you all the sauce you need.

---

preparing your fish
Scrape the fish from tail to head with the back of a knife to de-scale it, if required, then rinse. Cut along the length of the belly, open the fish and take out the innards, throat and gills. Use a spoon or the back of a knife to scoop up the blood vein from the backbone, then give the fish another good rinse. Done.

Valentine's lambs' liver kebabs

Sick of sausages and bored of burgers on your barbie? Well you've turned to the right page. Valentine Warner, champion of seasonal eating and star of *What To Eat Now*, brings us this delightful twist on barbecued kebabs.

Best day to serve this dish? Valentine's Day, obviously…

Serves 2–4

ingredients
250g of lambs' liver, sliced into strips (ideally about 3mm thick)
Salt
1 tsp of dried oregano
½–1 tsp of chilli powder
1 tsp of ground cumin
Vegetable oil
1 lime (juice only)
1 medium red onion, finely diced
A large handful of fresh coriander, chopped

method
Thread a few pieces of lambs' liver onto metal skewers (or wooden ones that have been pre-soaked so they don't burn on the grill).

Scatter the kebabs with a generous amount of salt, oregano, chilli powder and cumin before splashing a little vegetable oil over them. Grill the kebabs briefly over hot embers (wood smoke is essential) until coloured on both sides but faintly pink in the middle.

Before serving, pop the kebabs onto plates and squeeze over the lime juice, scatter with the raw onion and chopped coriander. Beautiful.

bush burgers

Make sure you use decent organic minced beef for this one. Adding sausage meat gives a really juicy, succulent burger and big chunks of yellow pepper will even make it look vaguely healthy.

Serves 4

ingredients

6 spring onions
2 yellow peppers
1 tbsp of olive oil
4 sausages
200g of minced beef
Salt & pepper

2 tbsp of chopped flatleaf parsley
8 rashers of streaky bacon (optional)
4 slices of mature cheddar cheese
4 burger buns
Salad
Ketchup or barbecue sauce-o-rama (p22)

method

Slice the onions and dice the peppers. Soften them in oil over a low to medium heat, then set aside. Slit open the sausages and squeeze the meat into a bowl. Add the minced beef, peppers, spring onions, salt and pepper and parsley and mix well.

Scoop out a little bit of burger mix and cook straight away to check the seasoning and adjust if required.

Now mould your burgers – the quantities here should make four fat, generous ones. Make a tiny hole through the centre of each patty. These will seal up when on the barbecue, but will ensure an even cook.

Put the burgers over a medium to hot heat and cook, turning occasionally. If you're adding bacon, cook the bacon at the same time and set aside.

When the burgers are nearly ready, lay a slice of cheese on each. If your barbecue has a lid, pop it down for a couple of minutes to help the cheddar melt.

Meanwhile, toast up your buns and get some salad chopped. Finally, assemble your burger, topping with some salad, a slice of bacon (if using) and then copious amounts of ketchup or barbecue-sauce-o-rama.

cool camping jerk chicken

This might just be our signature dish. Not because it's particularly original or fancy, but because we love it and cook it at every opportunity. It's a simplified version of a few different recipes given to us by various people, including Keisha. Hello, Keisha!

Serves 4

ingredients

4 tbsp of soy sauce
4 tbsp of Worcester sauce
4 tbsp of brown sauce
2 onions, grated
1 fresh green chilli (more if you like it hotter), deseeded & finely chopped
2 garlic cloves, peeled & crushed
1 tbsp of brown sugar – demerara is perfect
A handful of fresh thyme, finely chopped
Freshly ground black pepper
4 chicken breasts or thighs, de-skinned
Salad or rice, to serve

method

Mix all the ingredients, except for the chicken, together in a bowl. Make slashes across the chicken pieces to allow the flavours of the marinade to soak in, then cover the meat with the marinade and place it in a coolbox. Leave it for as long as possible to marinate.

When you're ready to cook, whack the chicken on a barbecue and cook evenly for around 20 minutes, turning regularly. Check the meat is cooked in the middle by inserting a skewer or fork into it – if it comes out piping hot then it's time to serve the chicken with salad or rice.

bags of salmon

Here's a delicious way to infuse shop-bought salmon (or other fish) fillets with oodles of flavour. Barbecueing the salmon in foil 'bags' helps keep them juicy and succulent; just add one of the four suggested flavour combos for a taste sensation, or feel free to experiment with interesting herbs and spice mixes.

ingredients

1 salmon fillet per person, plus your choice of flavours (see below)

fresh herbs and lemon:

Mix up 1 tbsp of olive oil, the juice of 1 lemon and a handful of fresh, chopped herbs like parsley, coriander, tarragon and chives. Add a little freshly ground black pepper and rub all over the fish. If you're out of herbs, add a splash of white wine to the lemon instead.

garlic butter:

Blend some softened butter with finely chopped garlic and fresh herbs. Wrap in foil and stick it in the coolbox. When set, add a couple of knobs to each fish bag.

pesto:

Smear some homemade pesto (p21) generously all over the fillet.

tomato and ginger:

Heat half a bottle of passata in a pan, grate in a thumb of ginger and add salt, pepper and a good pinch of sugar. Mix it all up, simmer for a few minutes and add to the bag.

method

Make a secure bag by taking a large sheet of foil, folding it in half, then turning over the two sides to make a wallet. Season the fillet with a little freshly ground black pepper and pop it into the bag with your choice of flavouring. Fold over the open edge of foil to seal the bag, then barbecue over a medium heat for 10 minutes. Fish doesn't take long and it's important not to overcook it, so peek inside the bag to check if it's cooked. When it's ready, it should be firm and no longer opalescent. If it's not, leave for another few minutes. Serve with some spuds and green vegetables.

sweet-chilli mackerel

When it comes to bathing in Thai sweet-chilli sauce, the MacKerel, above any other of the Scottish fish clans, just love it. Chuck a few spring onions into the tub, too, and you'll have the fish eating out of the palm of your hand. Or should that be the other way round?

Serves 4

ingredients

4 spring onions
A bottle of Thai sweet-chilli sauce
4 fresh mackerel fillets
4 large potatoes, peeled & cut into small chunks
2 tbsp of vegetable oil
Rocket and cherry tomato salad, to serve
Fresh flatleaf parsley and lemon halves, to garnish

method

Soak four wooden skewers in water so they don't burn on the barbecue (if you don't have skewers, you can stick the fish straight onto the barbecue). While they are soaking, finely chop the spring onions.

Drizzle the sweet-chilli sauce over the mackerel and then sprinkle on the onions, leaving the fish to marinate for 10 minutes.

Meanwhile, parboil the potatoes before draining them and adding to a pan with hot oil to sauté while you cook the fish.

Thread one fillet onto each skewer, then cook the fish, skin down, until nearly cooked (about 7 minutes, depending on the fillet size) then flip over and flash the meat side.

Serve the fish along with the potatoes and a fresh rocket and cherry tomato salad. And, for added flare, garnish with fresh flatleaf parsley and lemon halves.

Jubilate!

pork and apricot kebabs

Lots of flavour for very little effort – if only everything in life could be as simple. This is a happy, sunny little kebab. If it had a name, it would probably be called Pam.

Serves 4

ingredients

500g of pork fillet
24 dried apricots
Salt & pepper
Oil
3 tbsp of honey and/or mustard
Rice, pittas and salad, to serve

method

Slice the fillet into 2–3cm chunks and thread onto a large skewer, interspersing each chunk with a dried apricot. Season with a little salt and pepper. Paint the kebab with a little oil as well as the honey and/or mustard. Place over a medium to hot barbecue.

Turn regularly and brush with more honey and/or mustard every so often to keep the kebabs moist. You want the pork meat to be cooked through and the apricots to be nicely caramelised.

When ready, slide the pork and apricot off the skewer and enjoy with rice or pitta bread and salad. You could also try this with chunks of fresh apple if you're not keen on apricots.

jerk rum ribs

Rum and ribs might sound a little on the chalk and cheese side of things but, trust us, this unlikely combination will leave you lusting for more. So, unleash the caveman carnivore within you and revel in the silence while these chargrilled little beauties are gnawed into oblivion.

Serves 4–6

ingredients

Pre-made pot of jerked honey rum glaze (p22)
A packet of juicy pork ribs (so you have around 16 in total)

method

In a large bowl or flat dish, set your ribs to marinate in the sweet, sticky, spicy deliciousness of the glaze – though don't use all of it; keep some back for later. Leave them to soak up the flavours for as long as possible – we recommend about 30 minutes – turning them regularly.

Place the ribs carefully onto the sizzling barbecue, occasionally brushing over some of the marinade you put aside earlier. Turn them onto a new side when the cooked side has browned and charred. The average cooking time is around 15 minutes, though this depends on the heat of your barbecue.

Once they're done, slap them all on a plate and dig in – no cutlery allowed. This is finger food at its best – gnaw to your heart's content.

pork satay skewers

Peanuts and meat – who'd have thunk it? The fine people of the Far East, that's who. And how right they were.

The satay sauce used here is a little fiddly and needs to be made at home, in the presence of a food processor. This recipe also works well with chicken or beef.

Serves 4

ingredients

1 stem of lemon grass
1 medium fresh red chilli
1 garlic clove
1cm square of fresh ginger
1 tsp of groundnut or vegetable oil
1 small handful of fresh coriander

2 limes (zest & juice), plus extra to serve
225g of peanut butter
200ml of coconut milk
25g of soft brown sugar
550g of pork tenderloin

method

To make the satay sauce, peel and finely chop the lemon grass. Chop up the chilli and discard the painfully hot seeds, then peel and finely dice the garlic and ginger.

Pour the oil into a saucepan over a medium heat. Add the lemon grass, chilli, garlic and ginger and sauté for a few minutes. Separate the coriander stalks from the leaves, chop up the stalks and add these to the pan, along with the zest of one lime and the juice of two. Stir-fry for a few minutes, then add the peanut butter, coconut milk and sugar and mix until the sauce thickens.

Halve the mixture. Chop the coriander leaves into one half of the satay mix – this will be the dipping sauce. Cube the pork and stir it into the other half of the mixture. (If you're making it ahead of time, pop this into a food bag to marinate and keep cool, with the dipping sauce).

When it's time to cook, thread the pork onto metal skewers and smear with any remaining marinade. Place on a hot barbecue and turn occasionally until cooked through. Serve with the dipping sauce (hot or cold) and wedges of fresh lime.

spicy lamb koftas

These fiery little kebabs are delicious when served with a Moroccan-style salad, toasted pitta bread and some tangy minty raita. The more aggressive among you may also wish to note that they are wonderfully aerodynamic, especially when forcefully propelled towards the rear of a sworn enemy you have spotted sauntering past your campfire.

Serves 4

ingredients

500g of minced lamb
A handful of fresh coriander, finely chopped
1 onion, very finely chopped
1 fresh green chilli, deseeded &
  finely chopped
2 garlic cloves, peeled & crushed
1 tsp of turmeric
1 tsp of mild chilli powder
2 tsp of garam masala
1 tsp of salt

for the salad:
4 vine tomatoes, diced
1 green pepper, diced
1 yellow pepper, diced
1 cucumber, diced
1 red onion, diced
1 tbsp of lemon juice
A few fresh mint leaves, finely chopped
4 pitta breads

method

Soak eight wooden skewers so they don't burn on the grill, while you thoroughly mix together the lamb, coriander, onion, chilli and garlic. Add the turmeric, chilli powder, garam masala and salt and mix again.

Mould the meat into long sausage shapes around each skewer. Pop the kebabs onto the barbecue and leave to cook, rotating occasionally.

While the kebabs are cooking, knock up a quick minty raita (see p23).

To whip up a Moroccan-style salad, put the tomatoes, peppers, cucumber and onion in a bowl. Stir the lemon juice and mint leaves together and then drizzle over the salad. Toast the pitta breads and slice in half.

When the koftas are brown and sizzling, serve with the pitta, salad and minty raita.

campfire cuisine

Camping just isn't camping without a fire to warm your cockles, so light her up and try some of our fireside favourites. You'll find campfire classics alongside a few less-obvious recipes, but all taste sensational infused with flames and smoke you've created yourself.

First, a few words on campfire safety:

- Keep a shovel and a large bucket of water nearby.
- Build your fire at least 3m away from any trees, tents or undergrowth.
- Don't build a fire in the path of any strong winds.
- Avoid wearing loose clothing – a floppy sleeve will tempt flames.
- Never squirt liquid fuel on dying embers – unless, that is, you want to become a human firework.
- Keep your fire small and manageable.
- Make sure your fire is completely out before retiring to your tent. When it has died down, douse with water and stir with a shovel. Dig right into the centre and keep stirring until there's no more smoke or steam. Those hot coals are tenacious little buggers.

Right. Enough chat. Let's get building.

- Splinter two 30cm-long pieces of wood into a pile of kindling.
- Pile up a nice, tidy mound of shredded newspaper.
- Construct a tipi around the paper with the kindling.
- Lay over some light, dry branches, maintaining the tipi shape.
- Strike a match and touch it to the newspaper.
- Let the flames catch the kindling and then the dry twigs. Add a few more little twigs here and there.
- Gradually feed the fire with successively larger bits of wood. Go easy. Don't block air circulation by chucking a great big log on top of everything.
- Rejoice! For man hath created fire!
- To cook in or over the fire, let the wood burn down to a hot charcoal bed first. This should take about an hour.
- There will be hotter parts and cooler parts of the fire. Get to know which these are to help you expertly control your cooking times.

Most of the food in this section can sit straight on the coals of the fire, but a skillet (see p189) over the flames will give you more options. Adding a grill will allow you to tackle all the recipes in the barbecue chapter on your campfire, and with a big cooking pot or a Dutch oven (p13) there's no limit to what you can do.

wake-me-up omelette buttie

How do you like your eggs in the morning? We like ours with a kick…

This little beauty is just what you need to get you going bright and early. Well, it is eggsploding with spices, after all.

Serves 2

ingredients

3 rashers of bacon, cut into pieces,
  or a handful of pancetta/salami
2 tbsp of sunflower oil
1 onion, sliced
2 fresh chillies (red & green),
  seeds optional
3 garlic cloves, peeled & chopped
1cm square of fresh ginger, grated

½ tsp of turmeric
1 heaped tsp of ground coriander
1 heaped tsp of ground cumin
2 eggs
2 tomatoes, sliced
A handful of fresh coriander, chopped
Chapattis/pitta bread/crusty rolls/
  French stick – lovely bread

method

Fry the bacon in oil on your skillet or pan until the pieces turn irresistibly crispy. Remove a spoonful of the crispy bits for later and then add the onion, letting it soak up the salty juices and soften. Next up are the colourful chilli and garlic choppings – add and stir everything around for a couple of minutes. Sprinkle in the ginger and spices (it's handy to pre-mix them at home so you don't have to bring all the spice pots along with you) and cook until fragrant. Spread the mixture out evenly in the pan.

Beat the eggs in a bowl before pouring them over the mixture. Keep turning the omelette until it's cooked through.

Top with sliced tomatoes, the crispy bacon waiting patiently on the side and the handful of chopped fresh coriander. Serve the whole lot in a chapatti, pitta or crusty roll, or with a bit of French stick. Eggscellent.

sausage on a stick

The title says it all, really. But on a related note, did you know that 'pigsticking' was a blood sport popular in the early 1900s, where hunters with big moustaches galloped about on horseback spearing wild boars? Robert Baden-Powell, godfather of the boy scouts, was a big fan, apparently. Dib, dib, dib…

ingredients
Sausages
Bread
Tomato ketchup or barbecue sauce-o-rama (p22)

method
Find a stick. Make sure it's long and thick enough to be used as a toasting fork. Peel off the bark and sharpen the end. (You can also use wire or an old coat-hanger to wrap around your stick and double up on the sausages.)

Skewer your sausages and make sure they're well secured. Wipe the sausage with a little oil and hold over the fire. Keep turning regularly, until the snag is nicely browned and cooked through. Don't hold it too close to the flame or it will burn before it is cooked – be patient. When ready, use a slice of bread as an oven mitt to slide off the sausage, cover in ketchup or barbecue sauce-o-rama and devour.

skillet fajitas

Don't worry, readers – 'skillet' is just American speak for a frying pan or wok. They use lots of odd words, don't they? Like 'sidewalk', 'eggplant' and 'fanny pack'. Think of some more while you're knocking up these rather fine fajitas.

Serves 4

ingredients

Olive oil
1 bunch of spring onions, sliced
2 red peppers, sliced
2 yellow peppers, sliced
4 chicken fillets
Salt & pepper
A pinch of paprika
1 garlic clove, chopped
12 soft tortillas
200g of mature cheddar cheese, grated
1 small pot of sour cream

method

For campfire frying, you'll need a cast-iron skillet with legs to plonk over the flames (see p189 for stockists). Oil the skillet, then cook the onions and peppers over a medium to hot fire for a few minutes. Slice the chicken and add it along with a good pinch of salt and pepper. Add some paprika and garlic at this point, too.

Heat until the chicken is thoroughly cooked through and the onions and peppers are caramelised. Set aside, and heat up a tortilla in the pan. When it bubbles up, add some of the chicken mix, a good sprinkling of cheese and a dollop of sour cream.
Fold over and eat straightaway while good and hot. Like, awesome!

vegan pancakes

So, you think you know pancakes, huh? Think again. These are the badboys of the pancake world: monstrously fat, monstrously filling and monstrously fun for your little monsters to make. And they're vegan (see p18) too, thanks to Timothy Tang.

Serves 4 (2 pancakes each)

ingredients

500g of self-raising flour
1 tbsp of granulated sugar
1 tbsp of custard powder
700ml of soya milk
Much olive oil
Sweet topping of your choice: lemon juice, sugar, golden syrup or maple butter

savoury option:

Two or three asparagus tips
A handful of peas
1 shallot, finely chopped
A small handful of mint, chopped
A small handful of rocket
A few leaves of wild garlic
Salt & pepper

method

Mix together all the pancake ingredients in a bowl, leaving as few lumps of flour in there as you can. Put a decent amount of oil in the pan, then double it. Get it nice and hot before pouring in about an eighth of the mixture. Carefully swirl the pan around so that the mixture reaches the edges. When the pancake is solid enough to allow you to get a spatula underneath it, flip it over and fry for another minute or two, making sure that the mixture is cooked all the way through. (If you're the sort of person who throws ice cubes down the vest of danger, do feel free to toss your pancake in the traditional manner. Grass is good for you and a few blades can give this dish an added piquancy.)

Serve with whatever sweet option takes your fancy, or try the savoury option:

Toss the asparagus tips and peas into a pan of boiling water. Keep them there for a few minutes until the asparagus is just becoming tender. Fry the shallot (just one, but try to avoid saying 'that's shallot' – you'll be laughing alone) until it becomes transparent. Throw in all the other ingredients (including the drained asparagus and peas) and cook until well heated through and season according to taste.

Add the filling to the pancake mixture as soon as you have poured the latter into the frying pan and make your pancake as described above.

sweet stir-fry

Stir-frying food requires heat and speed – you can add practically anything to this recipe and it'll taste great. (Apart from hedgehog or porcupine, either of which will just give you a rather nasty case of 'spiny tummy'.)

Serves 4

ingredients

2 tbsp of olive oil
A bunch of spring onions, sliced
2 red or yellow peppers, sliced
200g of pork tenderloin, cut into medallions
2 tbsp of soy sauce, and more to serve
2 tbsp of runny honey
200g of mangetout

200g of fine green beans
200g of beansprouts
A handful of chopped fresh herbs, such as
   coriander, parsley or chives
2 lemons (juice only)
4 cakes of dried noodles
Sweet-chilli sauce (optional)

method

Get your skillet or chosen pan (and it should be the biggest you've got) over the fire so it's super-hot. While it's heating up, prepare your ingredients so you don't waste any cooking time. You want every ingredient you add to fry quickly, as opposed to a languid sauté. This means you may need to stir-fry each item individually, so have a warm bowl or dish handy to keep each item in when cooked.

Get your oil hot, and throw in the onions. Keep them moving in the pan. Then add the peppers – make sure they start to really colour. Now chuck in the pork, soy sauce and honey (transfer the veg into another pot or bowl, if necessary). When the pork seals, add the mangetout, beans and a little more oil. After a minute or two, add the beansprouts, herbs and lemon juice. Return any 'resting' veg to the pan and then give everything a hot, fast stir.

Serve on a bed of boiled noodles, adding more soy sauce as required. Some sweet-chilli sauce would give it a welcome kick, too.

Mamma G's spaghetti fish

Move over Rick Stein; our mate Charlotte's mum, Mamma G, is the new Codfather where gorgeous fish dishes are concerned. The beauty of this recipe is that you don't have to use a fresh fillet of fish (such as red mullet, mackerel, sardine, herring, cod or pollack); you can still knock up something super-tasty with tinned fish.

Give this one a go, just for the halibut…

Serves 4

ingredients

400g of dried spaghetti
4 small fish fillets
Olive oil
4 garlic cloves, peeled & finely chopped
Fresh or dried chillies to taste, deseeded & finely chopped
A huge handful of fresh parsley, chopped
Crème fraîche
1 lemon, cut into wedges

method

Cook the spaghetti first and keep some of the water to one side once you've drained it.

In the biggest frying pan you have, gently fry the fish in a little olive oil until it turns opaque and starts to flake. Add the garlic and chilli, turning the heat down to allow them to cook gently while the flaking fish picks up all of the flavour.

After a few minutes, add the parsley, crème fraîche and cooked spaghetti (if you can fit it in the pan, otherwise use a large bowl) and toss together just long enough to warm the spaghetti. If it starts to stick, add a little of the cooking liquid you set aside earlier.

Serve with lemon wedges and a drizzle of olive oil.

Leftovers taste delicious for lunch the next day, if you have the means to keep them cool.

calzone

Not exactly how Mamma used to make it – but then Mamma had a well-stocked kitchen, a large wine cellar and a goat called Alfredo tied to a lemon tree to help her. Pah.

Serves 4

ingredients

Ciabatta bread mix
A bunch of spring onions
Olive oil
1 tin of chopped tomatoes
Tomato purée
1 glass of red wine

Herbes de Provence
Plain flour
150g of ham, chopped
150g of mature cheddar cheese, grated
150g of mozzarella, broken into pieces
Salt & pepper

method

Unforgiving foodies may insist on crafting their own handmade dough, but in the wilds it's trickier, so go with the packet mix: make according to instructions and allow to rest.

Meanwhile, make the sauce. Simply chop the onions and fry in some olive oil. When softened, add the tinned tomatoes, a good squeeze of tomato purée and a splosh of red wine. Sprinkle with herbs, bring to the boil and allow to simmer until it thickens up.

When ready, roll the dough out into a flat circle about 20–25cm across (use flour so the dough doesn't stick). A wine bottle makes a perfect makeshift rolling pin. Take care not to roll the dough out too thinly – you don't want it to break when you add the filling.

Spread a good dollop of the tomato sauce over the pizza, add some chopped ham and cheese (half cheddar, half mozzarella), then season with salt, pepper and more herbs. Fold in half and seal up the edges, so it looks a bit like a Cornish pasty. Sprinkle some flour on a double thickness of foil and wrap up your calzone.

Rake the coals to give you a good flat layer and place the calzone on top. Cook for about 10–15 minutes, turning occasionally. Unwrap from the foil and enjoy, taking care not to burn yourself – the filling will be really hot.

Other fillings? Try chucking in a raw egg, mushrooms, chicken, olives, peppers… whatever you fancy, really.

building a tripod

The traditional way to support cooking pots and kettles over the campfire is to dangle them from a tripod. Making your own is easy if you have the raw materials to hand – and you'll look like a campfire expert! It's a blatant glory job, but it might just get you out of doing the washing up.

You'll need three strong branches or bits of wood, at least 1.5m long, and all roughly the same length. Lie two together on the floor in a tent shape with the top bits overlapping a small way, then bang a nail through the bit where they overlap, to secure them.

Stand them on end with the short bits sticking skywards, then use the third branch to complete the tripod, leaning it against the v-shape and tweaking the angles until it feels solid and secure. You can bang in another nail, if you like, but either way, some string or twine needs to be wrapped around the join until you're sure nothing will budge. (If you don't have a hammer and nails to hand, just use the string, but tie it extra tight.)

Before placing your finished tripod over the fire, douse it with a bucket of water to protect it from being burnt by the flames.

To support the cooking pot, you can either hang a length of chain from the centre of the tripod or use another length of wood. For the wood option, measure the drop from the centre of the tripod to the point at which you'll be hanging your pot. Don't forget to allow for the height of the campfire, the flames and the full depth of the cooking pot and handle. Your piece of wood should be longer than this, to stick out of the top of the tripod. Carve a good, big, angled notch out of the wood for the pot handle, then double-check the length before securing it to the top of the tripod with string.

For heavier pots, you may want to carve another notch at the top of the piece of wood; you can then feed the string through this notch when you secure it to the tripod, to stop it from slipping down into the fire.

veggie chilli on baked spuds

Aah, nothing like a steaming, buttery spud to lift any fireside meal from the desperate to the divine. Even more so when topped with this whip-crackingly tasty chilli. If cowboys had known about soy protein, they would have been all over this. Don't forget that potatoes on the fire always take longer than you think, so get 'em on early, partner.

Serves 6

ingredients

6 medium potatoes
Salt
Butter

for the chilli:
2 medium onions, chopped
Olive oil
3 garlic cloves, peeled & crushed
1 tsp of hot chilli powder
½ tsp of ground cinnamon

1 tsp of ground cumin
2 tins of chopped tomatoes
2 tins of red kidney beans, drained & rinsed
Water
225g of veggie mince (soy protein)
1 red pepper, cut into 1-inch squares
A dash of balsamic vinegar
2 tbsp of tomato purée
1 tsp of sugar
Grated cheddar cheese

method

Wash the potatoes, sprinkle lightly with salt and wrap individually with a double thickness of foil. Place the potatoes in the embers of your campfire and turn regularly for about 40 minutes.

Meanwhile, prepare your chilli. Using a large pan, fry the chopped onions in olive oil until soft. Stir in the crushed garlic followed by the chilli powder, cinnamon and cumin until all mixed together. Add the tins of tomatoes and kidney beans. Fill one-and-a-half used tomato tins full of water and pour into the pan.

Add the veggie mince and chopped red pepper and stir well. Mix in a dash of balsamic vinegar, the tomato purée and sugar. Bring to the boil and simmer for at least 10 minutes so that the mince cooks and the sauce becomes thicker. Stir occasionally.

When the spuds are soft and fluffy, carefully unwrap, cut open and fill with obscene amounts of butter, salt, cheese and piles of steaming chilli. Yee-hah!

Thai green curry

A fragrant, perky dish that's perfect for getting you out of the doghouse if you've been careless enough to be put in one. You'll need a nice big cooking pot to let everything slosh around in and to give everyone a go at stirring.

Serves 4

ingredients

250g of rice (basmati or long grain)
Groundnut or vegetable oil
1 tbsp of Thai green curry paste (p23)
A big thumb of fresh ginger, peeled & finely diced
1 fresh red chilli, deseeded & diced
A bunch of spring onions
2 red peppers

2 courgettes
100g of cherry tomatoes
2 tins of coconut milk
250g of tiger prawns
3 lemons or limes
A big handful of fresh coriander, chopped
Salt & pepper
Lime wedges, to garnish

method

First, put the rice on to boil, according to its packet instructions. Once it's simmering away, turn your attention to the curry.

Get a big pan, cooking pot or Dutch oven, add a good splash of oil and put over a medium heat. Add the curry paste, the finely diced ginger and the diced chilli. Slice and add the spring onions. Slice the peppers, add to the pan and allow them to soften.

Slice the courgettes and add to the pot, along with the cherry tomatoes. When the peppers have started to brown and the onions have softened, add the coconut milk and the prawns. Squeeze in the juice of the lemons or limes and stir well. Let this burble away for 5 minutes or so.

By now your rice should be practically cooked. Drain it, and add to the pot of curry. This will thicken up the sauce and allow the rice to absorb the flavours.

When the rice is cooked to your liking, stir in some chopped coriander, sprinkle with salt and pepper and serve garnished with some wedges of lime.

stewy dumpling delight

The key to this recipe is top-notch sausages, campers. Those cheapy ones from the corner shop will just disintegrate and turn to mush – and that'd be the wurst crime ever.

Serves 6–8

ingredients

6 good-quality big, fat pork sausages,
  chopped into pieces about 2cm thick
1 chorizo sausage, chopped into chunks
1 tbsp of olive oil
2 large onions, chunkily chopped
3 garlic cloves, peeled & sliced
2 red peppers, chunkily chopped
1 big sweet potato, chunkily chopped
1–2 tbsp of plain flour
2 tbsp of tomato purée
1 tin of chopped tomatoes
1 tsp of dried oregano
1 tbsp of paprika

1 tbsp of sugar
500ml of vegetable stock
Salt & pepper

for the dumplings:
150g of plain flour
75g of vegetable suet flakes
1 tsp of baking powder
A handful of fresh parsley, finely chopped
A handful of lightly toasted pine nuts
A handful of parmesan cheese, grated
Salt & pepper
7 tbsp of cold water

method

Fry the sausage and chorizo portions in a little bit of oil in a big pot or pan. Once they've browned, remove them and add the veg, cooking until it all starts to soften and colour. Sprinkle in the flour and add the tomato purée before giving it all a good stir and then letting the mixture cook for 1–2 minutes.

Tip the meat back into the pot, along with the chopped tomatoes, oregano, paprika, sugar and seasoning. Pour in enough stock so that all the ingredients are covered and you're left with a thin, stewy consistency. Give everything a good stir before bringing it to the boil, and then let it simmer for 15 minutes. Now add the dumplings (see opposite).

---

veggies
Substitute a can of butter beans for the sausages and a can of chickpeas for the chorizo.

To make the dumplings: place all of the ingredients, except for the water, in a bowl and mix well before pouring in a couple of spoonfuls of cold water at a time and kneading everything together with your hands – a sticky old job – until it suddenly comes together in a stiff dough. Roll the dough into individual balls, each about the diameter of a 50p-piece – this recipe should make roughly 12. Drop the dumplings onto the surface of the stew and push gently under with a spoon. Cover the pot and leave to cook for 30 minutes. Serve in a big bowl, with a large chunk of bread for dipping and a cold beer for sipping.

lemon chicken tagine

Brighten up even the dullest outfit by tipping this yellowy, fragrant, spicy dish over someone's head. Erm, hang on… is that right?

Serves 4–6

ingredients

1 tsp of garlic purée
Ground spices: ½ tsp of freshly ground black pepper, 1 tsp of ginger, a good pinch
  of saffron, 1 tsp of cumin, 1 tsp of turmeric, 1 tsp of cinnamon, 1 tsp of coriander
Olive oil
2 chicken breasts
12 chicken thighs
2 onions, chopped
200ml of water
250g of couscous
Salt & pepper
A handful of olives
2 lemons, sliced

method

This requires a bit of at-home prep or an early start at camp. Mix the garlic purée with the spices and a tablespoon of olive oil. Take the skin off the chicken pieces and de-bone the thighs. Cut the chicken into generous bite-size chunks. Mix these well in the spice mixture and refrigerate in a plastic bag wrapped in foil, or store in a coolbox.

When you're ready to get cooking, heat some oil in a saucepan, Dutch oven or suitable tagine dish, fry the chicken over a medium heat until sealed, then add the onions and continue to cook until they sizzle. Then add the water, put the lid on and cook over a low heat for about 20 minutes.

While this is cooking, prepare the couscous. Put it in a bowl with a pinch of salt and pepper, cover with boiling water and pop a plate on top. After 5 minutes, fluff the couscous up with a fork until the grains separate. Add it to the chicken mixture along with the olives and sliced lemons and stir. Add more water or some wine to get it to the consistency you want, heat through and serve.

the firepit

This is the most primal of cooking methods, and a sure-fire way to convince friends and family that you're but one step away from becoming one of those self-sufficient types who can live off the land and fashion a speedboat from two small coconuts.

You'll need space, time, a spade, bricks, chicken wire and some willing helpers.

Oh, and you need to start the whole process a good few hours before feeding time.

method

Right. The first thing you need to do is dig a big pit.

The size of the hole you need is determined by the size of what you're going to cook. The pit needs to be about 30cm larger in every direction than your total food area. Try a metre long and about half that in width and depth. Set aside any turf or earth you dig up carefully (because you'll need to put it back).

Now line your pit with bricks or stones. Bricks are a better bet, as they won't explode like flint and limestone.

Now build a large, well-fed fire in the bottom of your pit to make your charcoal cooking bed. You'll need a lot of hot coals for this, so if you're organised, you will already have a fire on the go from which to scoop some burning wood and charcoal for your pit. Ideally, you want the hot bed to be about 30cm deep.

While the fire's burning down (it should take about 3 hours), sort out the food you want to cook. You can be as ambitious as you like (we tried a duck stuffed with orange slices), but if it's your first time, go for uncomplicated stuff like a whole chicken, a juicy ham, a leg of lamb or hunks of beef. Vegetables like sweet potatoes, corn on the cob and butternut squash also react well to pit cooking, as they are difficult to overcook.

Season your ingredients well and wrap them in a generous amount of foil. Then wrap the foil packages in a heavy layer of wet newspaper or straw – this acts as an insulator to stop your food instantly frazzling. Now tightly mould chicken wire round each package so you can hook your food up later without burning your hands. Once the fire has burnt down, carefully lower in the food packages. Quickly refill the pit with soil and earth – the idea is to block off any oxygen from the firepit to keep the food from burning. Mark the pit area with sticks so you'll know where to dig later on, and leave for about 10 hours.

When you come back to the pit, dig up the covering (you need to be wearing protective gloves or oven mitts of some kind here), scrape off the ash and fish out your bundles of chicken wire. Carefully unravel to expose tender, moist treasures.

Eat, enjoy – and possibly beat your chest.

Obviously, a huge array of factors can affect cooking time – the size of your ingredients, how hot the coals are – so expect a little trial and error. But just think, when you get really good, you can try cooking a whole hog like the Polynesians do. Sure, it might take a week or so, but you can have one heck of a party while you're waiting.

pineapple flambé

Popular beat combo Crowded House once sang a song called 'Pineapple Head'. We wonder if they wrote it after too many nights on the rum punch, because we're still not sure what they were singing about. Ponder this while you roast your drunken tropical fruit – answers on a postcard, please.

Serves 4

ingredients
1 pineapple
Rum or your favourite spirit
100g of demerara sugar

method
Plonk your pineapple on a bed of hot coals, making sure you keep the leaves at the top out of the flames. Allow it to brown thoroughly all over. Then remove it from the heat and carefully slice away the skin, taking care not to burn yourself.

Return the fruit to the heat, make sure everyone stands well back, and pour over a healthy glug of rum. Flames will go everywhere, so watch your eyebrows. When the alcohol's burned off, grab the pineapple, pat on the demerara sugar and return to the heat, turning regularly until the sugar caramelises.

Hoist the pineapple by its singed leaves and carve off hunks of sweet, juicy, golden and rather boozy fruit... After eating several slices you'll be belting out the chorus for 'Pineapple Head', and understanding exactly what it's all about.

banana flakes

If there were an award for best fruit ever, then the banana would come pretty close to scooping it. This mellow yellow fruit is tasty, handily packaged and makes for a great comedy moustache. However, when Mother Nature created the banana, she forgot to include one very important thing… the chocolate!

Serves 4

ingredients
4 bananas
4 Flakes

method
Start to slice your chosen banana in half across its middle, but make sure you don't cut it right through. Snap a Flake in half, and carefully push each half down the middle of each banana handle. Lots of banana flesh will burst out – ignore it. And if the banana skin splits here and there, don't worry.

Manoeuvre the banana halves back together as best you can. Wrap snugly in foil.

Pop the bananas on the fire for about 5 minutes. Unwrap and scoop out the gooey, chocolately mess with abandon and delight.

comfort food

Sometimes, you get one of those days when everything seems to go wrong. A gale-force wind removes your hat. A goat nibbles through a tent pole. Your camping partner develops scurvy. You can't get that Westlife song out of your head. It rains, rains and rains some more.

These recipes are designed to give you a big, squishy hug when you're on the verge of burning your rucksack and heading for the nearest B&B.

Swiss breakfast

This is essentially what our friends in the North refer to as a hash – a comforting mush of leftover flavours to get your day going. Do the Swiss actually eat this for breakfast? Sadly, none were available for comment at the time of writing – but it would be nice to believe that they do.

Serves 2

ingredients
3 spring onions
2 tbsp of olive oil
4 rashers of streaky bacon
6 small boiled potatoes
Salt & pepper
4 slices of cheese
2 eggs

method
Chop up the spring onions and pop them in a frying pan with some olive oil over a medium heat. Slice the bacon, roughly chop the ready-boiled potatoes and add to the pan with a good pinch of salt and pepper.

Cook, meld and squish the mixture about until the onions have caramelised, the bacon is crispy and the potatoes have browned.

Add slices of cheese, allow them to melt and then split the whole lot between two plates. Fry up the eggs and balance on top of the mounds of hash.

Eat. Smile. Relax.

eggs in a hat

Not nearly as messy as it sounds, this dish covers all the comfort-food bases: mega yum; minimal mess; easy peasy! A delicious snack, not a fashion faux pas.

Serves 2

ingredients
Butter or oil
4 slices of bread
4 eggs
4 slices of cheese
4 slices of ham

method
Warm a frying pan, griddle or skillet and grease it well with butter or oil.

Use a drinking glass, empty jar or ramekin to cut out a circle in the middle of your bread. Place the holey bread on the griddle and lightly toast it on both sides. Crack an egg into the hole and cook until the egg white is almost solid.

Flip the whole thing over and put a slice of cheese on top, and then add a slice of ham. Serve when the cheese has melted.

Use the leftover bread circles to make the daintiest French toast ever!

minestrone soup

This is less of a soup and more a big bowl of hot, chunky, steamy, vegetable love. If it could, it would probably drive a VW campervan and listen to Creedence. Yeah, man. And don't Bogart that celery.

Some farm-fresh smoked bacon and a topping of sharp, tangy parmesan should give this all the punch it needs.

Serves 4

ingredients

1 tbsp of olive oil
4 rashers of bacon, rind removed, chopped (optional)
1 onion, diced
2 garlic cloves, peeled and crushed
1 celery stick, sliced
1 carrot, diced
1 courgette, diced
1 leek, sliced
2 tomatoes, chopped
500ml of vegetable stock
3 tbsp of small dried pasta shells
1 tin of borlotti beans (other beans will also do)
Salt & pepper
A handful of fresh parsley, chopped
A handful of parmesan cheese, grated
Crusty bread, to serve

method

Heat the oil in a pan and add the bacon (if using), onion and garlic. Sauté for a few minutes, then add the celery, carrot, courgette and leek and give it a good stir for 5 minutes or so over a medium heat. Add the tomatoes, vegetable stock, pasta and beans. Bring to the boil and then simmer for 20 minutes. Season to taste.

Serve in a bowl, and sprinkle over the parsley and parmesan. You'll probably need some crusty bread on the side to dip, scoop and dunk with.

multimillionaire's mushroom pasta

Named such because this recipe was first learned by Cool Camper no. 3 in the kitchens of an Italian multimillionaire's yacht. This *bambino* is quick, easy to make and if it's good enough for a multimillionaire and entourage…

Serves 4–6, depending on levels of greed

ingredients

1 onion
A generous pouring of olive oil
6 garlic cloves
1 pack of mushrooms (whatever type you fancy or can safely forage)
A big handful of fresh basil, torn up
2 vegetable stock cubes
2 small glasses of white wine

Salt & pepper
2 tbsp of crème fraîche, or cream if you want to go fatty
500g of fresh pasta (tagliatelle works really well, but you could use any type of pasta, fresh or dried)
Fresh spinach leaves
Parmesan cheese, grated

method

Chop up the onion and add to a frying pan with a very generous slosh of olive oil. As it's browning, add the garlic (diced or crushed), followed by all the chopped mushrooms and torn up basil leaves.

When the mushrooms have browned, crumble over the stock cubes and mix in, before adding the wine. As the alcohol cooks off, add salt and pepper then a couple of tablespoons of crème fraîche or cream.

Boil some water in another pan and add your fresh pasta (which should only take a couple of minutes to cook). Once it's ready, drain the pasta before heaping it all in with the sauce and give everything a good mix around. Then serve on a bed of spinach leaves and sprinkle some lovely grated parmesan on top – *bellissimo!*

feel-better bruschetta

Is everything looking grey, drizzly and a bit miserable? Bring a little Mediterranean sunshine to your plate with a quick, but utterly comforting, bruschetta. It's super simple, but with some ripe, juicy tomatoes, fragrant basil and homemade pesto, this toasty treat is absolutely sensational.

Serves 2 as a serious starter or a light lunch

ingredients

2 seriously good ripe tomatoes
100g of black olives (preferably ones that have been marinated in something exciting, such as garlic or chilli)
Fresh basil
2 tbsp of olive oil
Salt & pepper
Half a French stick
2 tsp of tapenade or pesto (for recipes, see Super-quick sauces, p21)

method

Cut the tomatoes in four, remove the seeds and dice the flesh. Take the stones out of the olives and chop them up any old how. Tear up the basil and mix everything together with most of the oil. Season with salt and pepper.

Cut off the knobbly end of your baguette and slice the rest of it lengthwise so you have two large, flat pieces of bread.

Rub the cut side with a little olive oil and toast it; spearing it on a couple of sticks over some hot coals will work just fine. Once it's toasted, spread the cut sides with a little tapenade or pesto. Then pile on the tomato and olive mix and devour, licking your fingers as necessary.

Chop and change your topping ingredients with anything you like – peppers, sliced ham, artichokes, grass… Okay, maybe not grass.

spicy sausage penne

Wherever you're camping, you'll always be able to hunt down a sausage. They travel in packs and don't run very fast. If you can't find plump, juicy organic sausages from a nearby local farm, supermarket ones will do for this recipe – but the thicker and herbier they are, the better.

Serves 4

ingredients

8 sausages (thick, herby and preferably organic)
Olive oil
2 onions, chopped
1 fresh red chilli, deseeded & chopped (optional)
2 garlic cloves, peeled & crushed
A glass of white wine
A handful of fresh oregano leaves, chopped, or 1 tsp of dried oregano
700g of passata, or 2 tins of chopped tomatoes
Salt & pepper
500g of dried penne
A handful of parmesan cheese, grated

method

Slowly brown the sausages over your grill, fire or frying pan. In another large pan, heat up some olive oil and sauté the onions, chilli and garlic for a few minutes. Cut the browned sausages into bite-size chunks and throw them into the mix with a splash of wine and the chopped oregano. Let everything bubble away for a few minutes.

Add the passata or tinned tomatoes and simmer for 20–30 minutes, stirring occasionally until the sauce thickens up. Season with salt and pepper.

Meanwhile, add the pasta to a saucepan of salted boiling water and cook until *al dente*. Drain well. Throw the pasta into the sauce and give it all a good stir, then serve up, with a generous sprinkle of grated parmesan.

Cobb pizza

We'd love to claim this *fantastico* pizza recipe as our own, but it's all thanks to the folk behind the Cobb Grill, and a similar recipe can be found in their *On The Go* cookbook.

Of course, if you don't have a Cobb Grill but you're staying at a campsite with its own woodfire pizza oven – you'll be surprised at how many have them these days – then pop your pizza in that, it tastes just as good cooked the old-fashioned way.

Serves 2

ingredients

1 ready-made pizza base (we know it's cheating, but you'll be oh-so-happy to just bust one out of its packet when you're tired after a day outdoors)
1 tasty jar of tomatoey sauce

1 fresh chilli, deseeded & finely chopped
1 ball of mozzarella, sliced
1 red pepper, diced
A handful of black olives
1 tsp of dried oregano
Fresh basil, chopped

optional extras:
Salami slices, anchovies, pre-cooked chicken pieces, mushrooms, cherry tomatoes, spinach leaves, maybe even some pineapple chunks – whatever you fancy.

method

Prepare the Cobb with the frying pan (you will need eight briquettes to heat it). Once the briquettes are lit, place the lid on top and leave it to heat up for about 7 minutes, while you make your pizza.

Smugly unwrap your pizza base and place before you – ta-dah! Then open up your jar of sauce and spread as many spoonfuls as you fancy (as evenly as possible) across the base, trying not to go over the edges.

Sprinkle over the chilli choppings before adding the slices of mozzarella and then pop the pepper pieces, black olives and a generous dusting of oregano on top of the cheese.

Once the Cobb is ready, place the pizza onto the frying pan and cook for 15 minutes or so, with the lid on. Add the basil, cut into slices and serve with a simple side salad.

Tucking into a bowl of this
steaming hot stuff feels as lovely as
a small elephant approaching you
on a cold, windy hill to give you a
comforting embrace and envelope
you in his large, velvety ears.

dry-your-eyes daal

The theory behind this dish is that you boil up the lentils in a pot, and in a separate pan fry up all sorts of spices. Then you chuck the sizzling spices into the lentil sauce – a method known as 'tarka', 'tadka' or 'baghaar' in Indian and Pakistani cooking.

Serves 4

ingredients

A cup of lentils: red or yellow
1 tsp of salt
A pinch of turmeric
1 lemon (juice only)
1 tsp of garam masala
1 tsp of chilli powder
Groundnut oil

1 onion, thinly sliced
1 tsp of ginger, either ready-minced or finely sliced
1 tsp of garlic, ready-minced or finely chopped
1 tsp each of cumin seeds and mustard seeds
1 fresh green chilli, deseeded & finely chopped
Fresh coriander
Naan, pitta bread or rice, to serve

method

Rinse a cupful of lentils three or four times and leave to soak for 20 minutes. The lentils will expand, so don't plonk too many in – it'll be trial and error depending on how thick or runny you want the daal to be. Rinse again and add enough water to just cover them. Add the salt and turmeric and bring to the boil. Cover and simmer for 10–15 minutes.

With a wooden spoon, fork or other sturdy utensil, stir the swollen lentils into a mush. When smooth, start trickling in water, stirring constantly, until you get the consistency you want – two or three cups of water should do the trick. Squeeze in some lemon juice, then add the garam masala and chilli powder before leaving to simmer.

In a shallow frying pan, heat up a generous amount of oil. Add the onion and fry until caramelised, then add the ginger, garlic, seeds and green chilli. These need to really sizzle and colour – make sure the oil is as hot as possible.

When the seeds are popping and everything's looking golden, stand back a little and tip the frying pan contents into the pot of daal. It will hiss and steam at you. Stir the tasty stuff through the gloopy lentils. Adjust consistency by either stirring in more water, or cooking down to a thicker sauce. Finally, tear some fresh coriander on top, and enjoy a bowl of daal with naan, pitta bread or rice.

camper's cassoulet

A rich, slow-cooked cassoulet, abundant with tomatoes, sausage, duck fat and beans, is the pride of many a kitchen in the south of France. Regional variations abound, each claiming to be more authentic than the other.

This, however, is a shockingly unauthentic version for you to hum and haw over as you sit by the fire. But it's dead easy, so is perfect for cooking on a gas burner.

If you're preparing this at home to freeze and use later, or are just feeling flashy, by all means use *confit de canard* instead of chicken thighs.

Serves 6

ingredients

6 chicken thighs, deskinned & deboned
1 heaped tbsp of duck or goose fat
  (olive oil will do, if you're stuck)
6 cooked sausages
5 garlic cloves
250g of chorizo sausage, cut into slices
1 tin of tomatoes

2 tbsp of tomato purée
A glass of white wine
1 chicken stock cube
2 tins of haricot beans
1 fresh bay leaf
1 sprig of fresh thyme
Fresh bread

method

Carve up the chicken thighs and fry in a little fat or olive oil. Slice the sausages, chop the garlic and add to the pan, adding more fat or oil as necessary to stop it sticking.

Throw in the sliced chorizo and stir.

Add the tinned tomatoes, tomato purée, wine, stock cube, beans (drained and rinsed) and herbs. Simmer for half an hour at least, stirring regularly. The longer you leave it, the tastier the stew will be.

Before serving, add any remaining goose fat to enrich the whole dish. Serve with big chunks of fresh bread.

roast chicken

This Sunday lunch staple is guaranteed to make everyone within sniffing distance go all misty-eyed and soppy. You do need a bit more kit for this, but if you don't have a Cobb Grill (p13) then a roasting barbecue with a lid will do the same job.

Serves 4

ingredients

1 medium-size chicken
Olive oil
1 head of garlic
1 lemon (juice & half the fruit)
Fresh rosemary or thyme (or dried

Herbes de Provence)
2 onions, halved
Vegetables (potatoes, sweet potatoes,
 parsnips, carrots, green beans, broccoli)
Salt & pepper

method

In a bowl or cup stir the olive oil with a couple of cloves of crushed or chopped garlic, a good squeeze of lemon juice and any herbs you may have lying about – fresh rosemary or thyme would be excellent, but dried Herbes de Provence will be fine.

Rub this oily, herby juice all over the bird – inside and out – before popping half a lemon, more herbs and half an onion into the cavity, and placing the chicken in the middle of the cooker or barbecue.

Chop your potatoes, sweet potatoes, parsnips and/or carrots into smallish chunks, give them a light coating of oil and arrange around the chicken with a few unpeeled cloves of garlic and any spare lemon or onion. After a final heavy sprinkle of salt and pepper, put the lid on and leave everything to cook for an hour and a half – occasionally checking on the chicken and shuffling a few spuds around to make sure everything's cooking nicely.

Shortly before the 90 minutes are up, get your other veg – broccoli, beans etc. – on the boil. To check that the chuck is ready, pierce a chicken thigh with a skewer – if the juice that runs out is clear, the bird is done. If the juice is even slightly pink, pop the lid down and let it cook on, keeping the veg warm in the meantime.

When cooked, serve the chicken with the spuds, roast onion and any other veggies you fancy. Don't forget to squeeze out the sweet roasted garlic flesh, and fish out the hot lemon from the chicken cavity – the juices will give you all the gravy you need.

hot chocolate

Like a hug from Stephen Fry or a big-eyed dog proffering you his paw, a cup of hot chocolate can make you realise that life isn't all that bad.

Serves 4

ingredients

2 pints of semi-skimmed milk
400g of milk chocolate
A bag of marshmallows
A can of squirty cream (optional)

method

Warm the milk in a pan, break up three-quarters of the chocolate into pieces and add this to the milk. Stir regularly to ensure the chocolate lumps don't stick to the bottom, until the chocolate has melted.

Pour the hot chocolate into four mugs or glasses and top with a marshmallow or two and plenty of cream, if you brought some along. Snap the remainder of the chocolate (or a chocolate stick of your choice; Flakes and Twirls go especially well) into four long pieces and use these as naughty edible stirrers.

something fancy

A good way to cajole reluctant campers into enjoying themselves is to exceed their expectations. By serving them up some lobster or a Sunday roast by the campfire, they'll see that cooking in the outdoors is not the preserve of strange men who collect roadkill. In fact, as these recipes prove, sometimes there's simply nothing posher. More champers, campers? Chin, chin!

Moroccan couscous with halloumi

What's gold and squeaky?

A 24-carat mouse? A suntanned guinea pig? No, no, no – barbecued halloumi, of course!

Serves 2

ingredients

1 mug of water
1 red onion
1 small aubergine
1 courgette
1 red pepper
2 tbsp of olive oil, plus a little more if you're
  frying the cheese

A pinch of dried chilli flakes
¾ mug of couscous
Salt & pepper
1 tsp of spice mix (Ras el hanout, Moroccan
  mix or allspice)
1 packet of halloumi cheese

method

Put a mug of water in a pan to boil and chop the onion, aubergine, courgette and red pepper into chunks. Heat half the oil in a big saucepan and add the chopped onion with a good pinch of chilli flakes, cook for a few minutes, then add the rest of the vegetables. Put a lid on, but stir it often and add a splash of water if it sticks.

While the veggies are cooking, prepare the couscous. Put the couscous into a bowl, add a little salt, 1 tsp of spice mix and the remaining oil. Mix well, then pour the boiling water over the couscous. Stir and cover the bowl straight away with a plate or anything to get a tight seal. Leave it alone with its thoughts for 10 minutes.

When the vegetables are nice and soft, but still shapely, take them off the heat and season well. Slice the halloumi cheese into thick slices and either grill on the barbecue or fry in a little oil until browned.

Uncover the couscous and fluff it up with a fork. Serve it with the vegetables and top with the gloriously golden and squeak-tastic halloumi.

salt-brick fish

This method may sound like utter madness, but we promise it works and won't leave you with a stupidly salty fish supper. Trust us. We love you like you're one of our own.

Serves 2

ingredients

2kg rock salt
4 egg yolks
Water
1 large fresh fish, gutted & cleaned (see p54)
1 lemon or lime, cut into wedges
Fresh herbs
Freshly ground black pepper

method

In a huge pan or bowl mix the rock salt with the egg yolks and enough water to turn the mixture into a congealed sludge.

Stuff your catch with a little lemon or lime, some fresh herbs and a grind of pepper.

Lay out a big double thickness of foil. Pour on a third of the salt. Lay the fish on top and then cover with the rest of the salt. Pat firmly together to mould into a salt brick, covering every last bit of the fish with salt.

Fold over the edges of the foil and wrap into a bundle. Pop in a Dutch oven (see p13) or lay straight on top of hot coals, covering with a few more. Leave for at least an hour and a half – if the fish is a real whopper, it may need longer.

When cooked, the salt should have hardened into a brick. Break it open to find your fish beautifully moist and cooked through inside.

baked lobster

Just think, if you were a member of the royal family you'd probably be able to enjoy a plate of baked swan with some fricasseed peasant on the side. But you're not, so you'd better make do with a spot of lobster instead.

Serves 2 as a starter or 1 as a main meal

ingredients
1 lobster
Butter, softened
1 lemon (juice only)
Lemon and garlic mayo (p21)

method
Ideally, you'll be selecting a fresh juicy lobster from the quayside near your campsite. If you're bringing one from home, you're better off carrying a frozen lobster in your rucksack than a fresh one (or a live one, come to think of it). It'll defrost through the day in your coolbox – just make sure it's fully thawed before you cook it.

Cut your lobster in half lengthways, from head to tail. Get rid of the brown stringy bit that runs down the tail, the feathery gills and the little green stomach sac.

Brush the lobster halves with soft butter and put them, shell side down, on a grill or hot coals for 3–4 minutes. You'll know it's ready when one of its small legs comes off with a gentle tug.

An alternative cooking method is to place the whole lobster shell side down on the grill or coals. Wait until the shell turns bright red, then turn and grill for another 5 minutes. When cooked, cut and prepare the lobster as above.

Drizzle lemon juice over the lobster, scoop out the white, sweet flesh and dip it into the mayonnaise. Crack the claws with the back of a heavy knife and savour the contents. Above all, feel smug that you are enjoying such a stereotypically snooty dish in the great wide open. Muwahahahaha.

seared tuna with rice Niçoise

We'll have none of that tinned tuna here, sonny Jim. That's for your cats and office lunches and motorway service stations, thanks very much. We only do fresh tuna here. If it's sustainable, like.

Serves 2

ingredients

100g of rice
2 hard-boiled eggs
A handful of fine green beans
Salt & pepper
2 fresh tuna steaks
Olive oil
A small handful of black olives
1 lemon (juice only)

method

Start by boiling your rice and eggs – set both aside when cooked. Trim the green beans and cook lightly by plunging in boiling, salted water for a few minutes.

Brush the tuna steaks with a little olive oil, then sprinkle some pepper on top of them. Sizzle the steaks over a hot barbecue or fry for a couple of minutes on each side, and then leave them to rest.

Mix the rice with the olives, a tablespoon of olive oil, salt and pepper. Spoon onto serving plates, artfully scattering over the blanched beans and peeled, quartered eggs.

Arrange the tuna steaks next to the rice salad and serve with a squeeze of lemon.

camper's Catalan stew

If you like to camp beside the seaside, get your hands on some fresh local seafood and bring a bit of Mediterranean sunshine to your plate with this deliciously fishy dishy.

Serves 2–3 if you're greedy, 4 if you're not

ingredients

A generous glug of olive oil
2 red onions, sliced
280g of chorizo sausage, diced
1 fresh red chilli, deseeded & finely chopped
1 red pepper, chopped
1 yellow pepper, chopped
2 garlic cloves, peeled & finely chopped
2 tins of chopped tomatoes
100ml of water

A large glass of white wine
A splodge of tomato purée
500g of firm white fish (such as pollock, cod or monkfish), cut into chunks
500g of mussels, cleaned
250g of raw king prawns, peeled
A bunch of fresh flatleaf parsley, chopped
1 lemon, cut into wedges
Crusty bread

method

Heat the olive oil in a large pan and fry the onions until softened. Add the chorizo and cook for a couple of minutes more. Add the chilli, peppers and garlic, and continue to cook for a further 2–3 minutes.

Pour the chopped tomatoes into the pot, along with the water, white wine and tomato purée. Leave this to simmer away for 5–10 minutes.

Add the chunks of white fish and bring back to a simmer. Discard any mussels that are open and do not close when tapped against a brick. Stir in the mussels and prawns, cover and cook for around 5 minutes or until the mussels are open and the fish is cooked. Discard any mussels that haven't opened.

Serve in a bowl sprinkled with lots of chopped flatleaf parsley and a lemon wedge. Mop up the juices with some lovely crusty bread.

mushroom risotto

Risottos soak up all sorts of flavours – so go heavy on the wine, fresh parmesan and herbs, keep a negligent eye on the clock and leave plenty of 'shroom in your tummy...

Serves 4

ingredients

2 onions
3 tbsp of olive oil
250g of mushrooms (a variety will make all the difference)
Salt & pepper
250g of arborio risotto rice
400ml of white wine
800ml of chicken (or vegetable) stock
50g of butter
100g of parmesan cheese, grated
A handful of fresh herbs of your choice, chopped
2 lemons or limes (juice only)

method

Slice the onions and soften in the oil. Hack up your chosen mushrooms and add – hopefully you've got a variety. Cook for a few minutes until the onions are softened and the mushrooms are browned. Season well with some salt and pepper.

Stir in the rice, cook for a minute or two and then pour in the wine. Bring to the boil and simmer, stirring the risotto regularly. As the liquid is gradually soaked up by the grains of rice, start adding the stock and continue to pour in more as it gets absorbed.

After about 20 minutes, the rice should be cooked and all the stock soaked up – add more water if you need it. Stir in the butter, grated parmesan and fresh herbs. Season with fresh lemon or lime juice, salt and pepper.

paella

As much a part of a trip to Spain as flamenco and siestas, paella is best enjoyed in the sunshine with a jug of sangria to wash it down.

Serves 4–6

ingredients

4 chicken thighs, deskinned and deboned
1 chorizo sausage
Olive oil
1 onion
1 garlic clove
2 red peppers, sliced
250g of mixed seafood (such as prawns, mussels, clams & squid)
200g of paella rice or arborio risotto rice
500ml of chicken stock
1 tsp of paprika
A pinch of saffron
White wine
4 limes

method

Chop the chicken and chorizo into bite-size pieces and fry with oil in the largest pan you can find. Dice the onion and garlic and chuck in along with the sliced peppers.

As the chicken browns, the onions and peppers soften and the chorizo goes crispy, add the seafood. Stir this around so that it seals and then put the mixture to one side.

Put the rice in a second pot with a tablespoon of olive oil and cook for a couple of minutes. Pour in the chicken stock, then add the paprika and saffron. Bring to the boil and simmer, stirring regularly. The rice should start to soak up the stock. Add a good slug of white wine. When the rice has cooked, tip it in with the meat and fish. Stir everything well and bring the heat back up. Slice the limes and stir these in – then serve up. *Olé!*

lamb chops with couscous

Couscous grains are quite tiny, measuring just 1mm in diameter once cooked. Which is small to us, but quite big from an ant's point of view. Think about it.

This delicious, colourful dish benefits from heavy-handed seasoning and a dollop of the minty raita on p23.

Serves 4

ingredients

4 lamb chops
2 tsp of ground cumin
4 tsp of garam masala
Salt
Olive oil
200g of couscous
1 red onion, chopped
1 fresh chilli, deseeded & finely chopped

A handful of fresh thyme
3 peppers: red, yellow & green, diced
1 courgette, diced
Freshly ground black pepper
A handful of fresh parsley, chopped
15 cherry tomatoes, halved
1½ lemons (juice only)
Minty raita

method

Marinate the lamb chops in the cumin, half the garam masala, a teaspoon of salt and a little olive oil. Leave to marinate for as long as you can manage. Then barbecue to suit your taste – charred on the outside and pink in the middle suits us just fine.

Meanwhile, tip the couscous into a pan of just-boiled water – you want the water level to be about 2cm above the couscous. Cover for 5 minutes.

Pour some olive oil into a frying pan and cook the chopped onions until they soften. Add the chilli, thyme, peppers and courgette. Stir in the remaining garam masala and let the vegetables brown a little here and there.

Add the couscous to the frying pan, season heavily with salt and pepper and mix it all together thoroughly with the vegetables.

Add the parsley, tomatoes and the lemon juice. Serve up the couscous with the lamb chops and a dollop of minty raita.

Sunday roast beef

As British as cucumber sandwiches and fights outside pubs at closing time, a roast beef dinner is the pride of the nation. This barbecue-based beef-fest is so special you'll want to take a picture of it to keep in your wallet.

Serves 4

ingredients

500g rib of beef
Olive oil
Salt & pepper
Herbes de Provence
8 shallots or 4 onions, skins left on

12 medium-size potatoes
4 courgettes
4 peppers: 2 red, 2 yellow
Horseradish sauce, to serve

method

Rub the beef with a little oil, salt and pepper and a tablespoon or two of Herbes de Provence. Start to cook slowly over a medium-heat barbecue, making sure you keep turning it. Someone will need to perch near it for the next hour or so to keep it from burning or cooking too quickly.

Put the shallots or onions onto the barbecue and turn regularly until they caramelise.

Meanwhile, boil the potatoes. When they're cooked, drain the water and sprinkle the potatoes with a little salt. Barbecue these until they start to brown up and go crispy. Once the potatoes and shallots are cooked, put them to one side, wrapped in a dry tea towel to keep warm.

Chop the courgettes into 3cm sections and cook them on the barbecue along with the whole red and yellow peppers.

The beef is cooked when a skewer that's been pushed into the centre of the meat for 3 seconds comes out hot. Test it on the inside of your wrist. Once it's cooked, leave the beef to rest for about 15 minutes. In the meantime, pop the potatoes, onions, courgettes and peppers onto individual skewers and return to the barbecue to get them nice and hot.

Carve up the beef and enjoy with the barbecued trimmings – a little horseradish sauce would top the plate off nicely.

a bit on the side

Whether you need a quick snack to keep the wolf from the door, want to add some extras to a barbecue or wish to extend a little hospitality after an unexpected visit from a large walking tour, here are a few extra recipes for you and your guests to enjoy.

paneer and vegetable kebabs

Hailing from India, paneer cheese is a bit like mozzarella – but it won't melt during cooking, making it ideal for barbecues. We think it's a bit underrated, but once you've tried these barbecued cubes of cheesiness, there's no going back...

Serves 4

ingredients

1 tbsp of olive oil
1 lemon (juice only)
A handful of fresh basil, finely chopped
1 garlic clove, peeled & crushed
Salt & pepper
8 button mushrooms, halved

2 courgettes, sliced thickly
2 red peppers, cut into chunks
2 green peppers, cut into chunks
2 yellow peppers, cut into chunks
2 red onions, cut into quarters
1 box of paneer, cut into large pieces

method

Mix the olive oil and the juice of a lemon with the chopped basil and the crushed garlic. Season with salt and pepper. Place all the vegetables and the cheese in a bowl. Pour over the marinade and leave for 15 minutes.

Thread alternate chunks of vegetable and paneer onto 8 wooden skewers (that have been pre-soaked), using two pieces of cheese per skewer.

Place the kebabs on the barbecue and turn them frequently so the vegetables and cheese cook evenly. Brush the kebabs regularly with the leftover marinade. Once the veggies have cooked through and the cheese has browned, serve with barbecued meat, couscous or a salad.

superfood smash

Here's another easy-(chick)peasy bit on the side that'll go with just about anything, or you can serve it alone as a healthy snack – hot or cold.

Both chickpeas and spinach count as superfoods, in case you didn't know. So this'll give you a double health hit.

Serves 2–4

ingredients

2 tbsp of olive oil
1 white onion, chopped
4 garlic cloves, peeled & crushed
1 tin of chickpeas, drained & rinsed
1 tin of spinach (or you can use fresh leaves, if you have them)
Salt & pepper
Chilli powder (optional)

method

Heat the oil in a pan and cook the chopped onions, leaving them to soften a little before you add the crushed garlic. When the onion and garlic are soft and just starting to colour, add the chickpeas and cook for about 5 more minutes – stirring constantly. The chickpeas should now have softened sufficiently for you to start mushing them up with a fork or potato masher.

Mash away until the mix is a kind of 'smash', and then add the spinach and salt and pepper (and possibly a teaspoon or two of chilli powder) to taste. Give the smash a big stir before serving in a bowl or as part of a main meal.

hot halloumi salad

The mountain peoples of the remote Greek island of Gregoriakis greet the arrival of every newborn infant by constructing a giant ceremonial trumpet using only a mountain of halloumi cheese and a barrelful of chest hair.*

While that's all very well and good, we've decided to use our halloumi to make this hot and tasty salad instead. Though you could always build a mini-Stonehenge out of yours, if you're feeling bored.

Serves 4 as a side dish, or 2 as a main meal

ingredients

2 lemons (juice only)
1 fresh red chilli, deseeded & finely
  chopped
Olive oil
1 packet of halloumi cheese
1 yellow pepper, diced
1 red pepper, diced
Fresh mint, chopped

Fresh thyme, chopped
Freshly ground black pepper
1 packet of salad leaves – rocket is ideal
A handful of green or black olives
1 red onion, chopped
1 Lebanese cucumber, peeled and cubed
  (a regular cucumber will do)
250g of cherry tomatoes, halved

method

Squeeze the juice of one lemon into a bowl. Add the chopped chilli and some olive oil.

Cut the halloumi into slices and sprinkle the marinade over it. Leave it for 30 minutes, or longer if you have time. Place the peppers and the halloumi onto the barbecue and turn frequently until the cheese becomes golden brown on both sides and the peppers turn a rich dark colour. Leave to cool.

For the dressing, blend the chopped mint and thyme with a healthy slug of olive oil and the juice from your second lemon – add a grind or two of black pepper too.

Mix the salad leaves, olives, onion, cucumber and tomatoes into a large bowl. Add the barbecued halloumi and peppers and give everything a light jumble. Drizzle over a generous glug of the herby dressing and serve.

* This is a lie. Sorry.

damper bread

This is unhygienic, unhealthy and horribly messy. The kids will love it.

Serves 8

ingredients

600g of self-raising flour
100g of caster sugar
A pinch of salt
100ml of water
A filling of your choice, such as jam, butter, honey, cream or chocolate spread

method

Mix the flour with the sugar and salt, and blend with some water to form a dough. Knead lightly until smooth, and allow to rest somewhere cool for 10 minutes or so.

Meanwhile, sharpen a long, sturdy stick, taking care to scrape off the bark.

Take a small handful of the mixture and squish it onto the end of the stick so it looks like a thick sausage.

Cook over the fire, turning regularly until it swells, browns and feels solid when you tap it.

Carefully pull the hot damper bread off the stick and fill the hollow with jam, butter, honey, cream, chocolate spread or anything else that takes your fancy.

Med veg

A sweet, colourful accompaniment to just about anything – enjoy on toast, stirred through pasta or with a juicy lamb chop. Cook these on site or rustle them up beforehand and allow them to marinate in their own juices.

Serves 4

ingredients
2 red onions
4 sweet peppers
4 courgettes
1 aubergine
A head of garlic
Olive oil
Balsamic vinegar
1 small bunch of fresh rosemary, chopped
Salt & pepper

method
Chop, peel and slice your various vegetables so that everything's vaguely the same size. Break the garlic head into cloves, but keep them in their skin (they'll get lovely and sweet inside it during cooking). Coat everything with a generous amount of olive oil, a shake of balsamic and a scattering of chopped rosemary. Season to taste.

If time's on your side, you may as well barbecue everything. It's a bit fiddly and takes a while, but the veg will smell great and develop pleasing black char lines.

Pop the garlic cloves on a little foil tray so they don't escape through the wires.

If you plan on cooking this at home, heat a large baking dish in the oven at about 180°C (gas mark 4) with a generous splosh of olive oil. When it's hot, throw in all the vegetables and the rosemary. Mix around well and season with salt, pepper and balsamic vinegar. Cook for an hour, shaking the tray around every 15 minutes or so to ensure an even roast. Allow it to cool, then refrigerate, ready for your camping trip.

vegan couscous tabouleh

Nope, this isn't an obscure dance at a Big Fat Greek or Gypsy Wedding, but a healthy vegan (see p18) meal or super side dish. And the presentation options go on and on and on (much like a Big Fat Greek or Gypsy Wedding)...

Serves 4

ingredients

A large bunch of fresh flatleaf parsley (or dandelion leaves will do), finely chopped
In spring/early summer, add a handful of wild garlic, roughly chopped
2 tbsp of fresh mint, finely chopped
4 spring onions, finely chopped
4 medium tomatoes, finely chopped

2 lemons (juice only)
4 tbsp of olive oil
Salt & pepper
100g of couscous
125ml of water
1 vegetable stock cube
1 tsp of dried mixed herbs

optional extras:
Lettuce leaves or halved red or orange peppers, for groovy presentation

method

Once you've chopped up all the herbs and veg, use your knife to slide them gracefully off the chopping board into a nice big mixing bowl. Squeeze the lemon juice over the top before drizzling in the oil and adding salt and pepper to taste.

Sprinkle the couscous into a saucepan and pour in the water, adding a cube of vegetable stock and the mixed herbs. Bring it to the boil then simmer for a couple of minutes. Set the pan to one side for 5 minutes before scooping the couscous into the bowl with the rest of the ingredients and mixing everything together.

Then take endless photos of it with lettuce leaves in various presentational poses that seem disappointing at the time but turn out okay.

garlic bread

Nothing gets folk salivating faster than garlic bread. If you wanted to, you could tie some to a long stick, wave it around and watch people scamper after it.

Serves several

ingredients

150g of butter
2 garlic cloves, peeled & crushed
A small bunch of fresh parsley, finely chopped
Salt & pepper
1 loaf of bread

method

Cream the butter in a bowl, squish in the garlic crushings and stir in the parsley with a good pinch of salt and pepper.

Cut the loaf into thick slices and toast over a fire or in a frying pan. Once one side is toasted, spread it generously with the butter then toast the other side, allowing the butter to melt right through. Scoff while hot, crispy and dripping with garlicky goodness.

George's smackerel of mackerel

And if that's not enough for you, why not try adding a smackerel of mackerel, like our friend George does? You'll need a tin of mackerel – or, heck, maybe even sardines if you really want to let your hair down – a bottle of tabasco and a few rocket leaves.

Just top your slice of garlic bread with as much of the above as you fancy or can fit onto the bread. It makes a super-easy snack while you're on the go, or a starter to snaffle down when you're cooking up a storm over the campfire. George likes to have it as an awesome camping brekkie with a strong black coffee, but he's crazy like that.

sweets & treats

Would life be worth living if you couldn't settle down now and then to enjoy a biscuit, or maybe a cake, with a nice cup of tea? No, quite frankly. Every so often, you can't beat a bowlful of something sweet, sticky and possibly quite bad for you.

The following recipes have been vaguely split into two camps: delicious things you'll need to make at home (see p171–174), and the rest are all goodies you can concoct in the wilderness.

baked bananas with giant ginger biscuits

Mmm... a crunchy, gungey, flongey, squodgy, flupperly delight. Yes, those are real words.

Serves 2 (but you'll have 6 biscuits in total, so there'll be 2 spare for midnight munchies)

ingredients

60g of butter
75g of caster sugar
185g of golden syrup
2 tbsp of treacle

3 tsp of ground ginger
300g of self-raising flour, sifted
2 bananas
Peanut butter or chocolate (optional)

method

Biscuits first. Pop a saucepan over a low to medium heat and add the butter, sugar, golden syrup, treacle and ginger. Stir until the butter melts and the sugar dissolves. Remove from the heat and leave to cool.

When the treacle mix is at room temperature, stir in the sifted flour a little at a time. This will become pretty tough going as the goo stiffens up, but persevere.

Take pieces of dough the size of small oranges, roll each into a ball, slightly flatten down and arrange on baking trays covered with greaseproof paper. You may need a few trays, as you might only get one on each, depending on the size of your biscuits. If you are arranging more than one on a tray, leave about 5cm between the biscuits as they will spread out. Bake the biscuits in a preheated oven at 190°C (gas mark 5) for about 12–15 minutes until they are golden, then use a spatula to remove them from the tray.

Cool on a wire rack, and store in an airtight container. Over time they may become a little chewy, but this is all to the good.

Now for the bananary bit. Cook the bananas in their skin straight over hot coals or on a barbecue. When the skin blackens, pop the banana onto a plate and carefully slice open lengthways. Crumble the ginger biscuits and sprinkle liberally over the hot banana.

A little peanut butter or chocolate wouldn't do any harm here, either.

stickified goo-goos

Crazy name, crazy recipe. Seriously, the sugar buzz off these badboys is enough to give you hairy palms.

Serves 8–10

ingredients
100g of butter
1 packet of butter toffees
1 packet of marshmallows
3 handfuls of puffed rice

method
Put the butter, toffees and marshmallows in a pan over a low to medium heat. Stir regularly until you have a scary-looking, sticky mass. Pour in the puffed rice and mix together.

Using a wet spoon, dollop the goo by the spoonful into paper cases. Let them set in the refrigerator or coolbox, then store in an airtight container. Don't stack them on top of each other, else it'll just turn into an unsightly mess.

When they are set you can eat, enjoy, then run around a field whooping…

chocolate cement

This stuff has the power to turn cloud into sunshine, frowns into smiles and bad-tempered campers who've forgotten essential hair maintenance items into beaming, delightful outdoor companions.

Serves 4

ingredients

140g of dark chocolate
4 egg yolks
185ml of double cream
4 heaped tbsp of cocoa powder
2 tsp of orange zest

method

Break the chocolate into pieces and melt in a bowl set over a saucepan of simmering water, making sure the bowl doesn't touch the water. When it's nice and runny, beat in the egg yolks (make sure they're at room temperature before you add them so that they don't cool the chocolate down).

Beat the cream, cocoa powder and orange zest together until the mixture forms stiff peaks, and then fold it into the chocolate. Pour the lot into a container and refrigerate for a good 12 hours before you need it.

This'll leave you with a solid dishful of chocolate goodness to spoon out and enjoy when you're atop a hill, leaning on a tree, hiding in a cave… or just sitting on the sofa.

s'mores

Okay, so this is the British version of a classic American campfire treat. Anything they can do, eh? Plus you don't have to use Hersheys. Bonus.

Serves 4

ingredients
A packet of digestive biscuits
A couple of your favourite choccy bars, chopped up into slivers
A bag of marshmallows

method
For each s'more, take two digestive biscuits and lay pieces of the choccy bar on top of one. Toast a marshmallow (or two) to gooey perfection on the campfire or barbecue.

Place the melted marshmallow(s) on top of the choccy, before squishing the second digestive biscuit on top to form a deliciously gooey sandwich. This is probably the best creation known to man.

Once you've done one, do s'more.

chargrilled peaches and honey

The Stranglers did a song called 'Peaches', didn't they? But it wasn't about how lovely peaches are. Oh no. It was about bums. How rude.

Serves 2

ingredients

4 peaches
Honey
Cream (optional)

method

Put the peaches on a grill over a hot barbecue or fire embers. If they're not totally ripe in the first place, cut them in half and remove their stones before putting them on the fire. Cook until their skins blacken and their flesh softens.

Then slice the peaches and pour over ridiculous amounts of honey. We suspect some cream would be good here, too.

berry baked apples

An autumnal favourite, especially if the apples have been recently hoiked from their tree and the blackberries are freshly picked. If you've got some cinnamon to hand, that'd just be extra-cosy.

Serves 4

ingredients

4 cooking apples
Ground cinnamon (optional)
2 handfuls of blackberries
Cream, to serve (optional)

method

Score a line around the waist of the apple to prevent it from splitting and exploding. Partially core it, leaving about 1cm of apple at its base. Sprinkle over a little cinnamon, if you have any, then fill the hole by squishing in as many blackberries as possible. Wrap the lot in foil and rest in the embers of the campfire. Cook for 20 minutes, turning the foil-wrapped apples regularly.

When ready, the apple should be a golden-brown, giving up fluffy, crimson-stained flesh. Carefully unwrap and serve with lots of cream, if you like, and any leftover blackberries.

marinated oranges

Oranges are good for you. Grand Marnier isn't. Put them together for a naughty-tasting, healthy-looking treat. These oranges are quite boozy, so don't give them to any kids unless you want Social Services on your case.

Serves 2–4

ingredients
6 oranges
2 shots of Grand Marnier
75g of dark chocolate, grated

method
Take a sharp knife and cut the tops and bottoms off the oranges. Now peel the skin off your central lump of orange, leaving you with a messy piece of flesh. Cut into segments over a bowl, so you catch any dribbles of juice.

Add the Grand Marnier to the segments, cover and refrigerate or stick in a coolbox.

When you're ready to serve the marinated oranges, sprinkle them with the chocolate shavings and tuck in.

orange-baked muffins

Did you know that by hollowing out a humble orange you get a sensational disposable cooking vessel? It's true – throw out your frying pans! You can always use shop bought muffin mix if you don't want to make it yourself. We won't tell.

Serves 6

ingredients

6 oranges
100g of plain flour
80g of butter
1 egg, beaten
80g of brown sugar
80ml of milk
2 tsp of baking powder
1 tbsp of cocoa powder

method

Cut the top off each orange and keep the 'lid' to one side. With a sharp knife, thoroughly hollow out the fruit, eating the flesh as you go. Check there are no holes elsewhere in the orange peel – plug them up with a bit of pith if there are.

To make the muffin mix, sift the flour into a bowl, add the butter, egg and brown sugar and give the mixture a really good stir. Add the milk and baking powder, then sift the cocoa powder in and stir again until the mixture is blended together nicely. Using a whisk helps to mix it all up good and proper.

Stuff the mixture into the empty orange shells so they're about half full. Put the lid back on each and wrap well with foil.

When you've run out of muffin mix (or oranges), place the silver globes onto hot coals and leave for about 20 minutes, turning now and then. Don't be afraid to unwrap one carefully to check on progress. When you think they're cooked, remove from the heat and wait for them to cool a little before you handle them. Then unwrap, discard the lid and spoon out the warm, orange-tinged muffin.

tin cakes

We're all for recycling here at Cool Camping HQ, and if recycling tin cans means you can make cakes in them, then sign us up!

So it's not 'cooking' per se, but kids love watching the cake mixture rise up in the cans and... overflow like lava from a chocolatey volcano if you happen to have overfilled yours. Ahem.

Serves 6

ingredients

1 packet of cake mix
Whatever the cake mix packet demands – usually eggs, milk and water.

method

Mix up your cake mix according to the packet instructions, then carefully line six washed tin cans with foil – cunningly saved from other camping meals like the Four-Can Stew (p48). Check that there are no holes in the foil before you pour in the mixture (otherwise you might end up with burnt cakes), half-filling each can.

Pop a little foil lid on top of your cans before placing them around the very edges of the fire, turning regularly until a penknife, whittled stick or skewer prodded in the middle comes out clean.

Whose cake will rise the highest? The campfire gods will decide.

stuff we like

We've done a fair bit of cooking to get this book shipshape, and although we would love to take all the credit for the delicious finished dishes within its pages, many of the recipes featured wouldn't have turned out quite so tasty were it not for a helping hand from the following camping gadgetry wonders. We suggest you leave the book open at this page a week or so before your birthday. Maybe even circle the things you especially fancy!

Corn on the cob? How about everything on the Cobb!

This pioneering roaster-steamer-smoker from Cobb is a kitchen on the go. It may not wash your dishes, but will cook just about anything, including a better-than-your-mum's roast chicken.
www.cobb-bbq.co.uk

Come on baby

Light My Fire offer a giant range of uber-stylish camping accessories. Choose from funky mess tins to nifty fire-starting kits and, of course, the revolutionising and legendary sporks.
www.lightmyfire.se

What's cooking?

Talk to the nice people at Eddingtons for cast-iron cookware, Dutch ovens and one of our best-loved cooking gadgets, the Diablo, which makes delicious toasties in a hurry.
www.eddingtons.co.uk

On the boil

For a novel way of making a brew, check out Eydon's storm kettle. It can be lit with a piece of paper and you can use anything that burns, including camel dung if you have some spare…
www.eydonkettle.com

Breakdown barbecue

This amazing barbecue grill from Grilliput folds down into a neat little tube not much bigger than the size of a large cigar – perfect for a lightweight camping trip.
www.grilliput.com

Campfire on wheels

Camping isn't camping without a crackling fire on the go, but burnt holes in the grass don't make for a pretty campsite. At last we have the perfect solution for campsite owners and campers alike. A firepit you just pop in the ground, light and enjoy.
www.somersetfirepits.co.uk

It's a skillet, innit

A skillet, like this one from Nordic Outdoor, is one of the most effective tools for cooking over a campfire. Not only does it look wonderfully rustic, it's versatile – pop pots on it, too – easy to use, and cooks everything super-quickly and super-tastily.
www.nordicoutdoor.co.uk

Chilling grilling

One of Cool Camping's faves, a Campfire Cooking Grill should belong to every camper. It swivels to suit your cooking needs and can be adjusted to fit any campfire, stove or firepit.
www.campfirecookinggrill.co.uk

Gaz-tronomical

Don't get heated looking for the perfect stove; the folk at Camping Gaz have a stove for every camper and occasion, whether you're after a 2-hob-plus-toaster or a lightweight single backpacker stove.
www.campingaz.com

Top notch

We've all done it: lovingly prepared a prawn or scallop and gently placed it on the barbie, only to watch helplessly as it falls between the grill to meet its fiery end. This clever barbecue topper puts an end to these harrowing tales. Part of Lakeland's summer range.
www.lakeland.co.uk

index

Share your food!

We hope you enjoyed the *Cool Camping Cookbook* and have learned a few new things for your next trip. If you have your own special camping recipes, why not share them with us? We'll credit all the recipes we receive – and the best contributions will be awarded with a free copy of the next *Cool Camping Cookbook* in which the recipe will be printed. Send your recipes to **food@coolcamping.co.uk**

The *Cool Camping Cookbook* (2nd edition)
Series Concept & Series Editor: Jonathan Knight
Recipes & Writing: Tom Tuke-Hastings,
Nadia Shireen, Shellani Gupta, Jonathan Knight,
Dave Richards (aka the Barefoot Chef),
Harriet Yeomans, Amy Sheldrake, Sophie Dawson
and Dixe Wills
Editor: Sophie Dawson
Proofreaders: Leanne Bryan, Nikki Sims,
Catherine Greenwood
Design & Artwork: Nicola Erdpresser,
Harriet Yeomans
Cover Design: Kenny Grant
Publishing Assistant: Amy Sheldrake
PR: Shelley Bowdler

Published by:
Punk Publishing Ltd, 3 The Yard,
Pegasus Place, London SE11 5SD

Distributed by:
Portfolio Books, 2nd Floor, Westminster House,
Kew Road, Richmond, Surrey TW9 2ND

All photographs © Tom Tuke-Hastings,
Jonathan Knight, Harriet Yeomans, Amy Sheldrake,
Shelley Bowdler, Dixe Wills, Sophie Dawson, except
the following, reproduced with kind permission: p36
© Dave Richards; barbecue topper p189 © Lakeland.

Front cover © Harriet Yeomans

Thanks and love:

Big thanks to the following for help and support above and beyond the call of duty: Wapsbourne Manor Farm (www.wowo.co.uk) for letting us cook up a storm at their super site; Dixe Wills for some champion washing-up skills, presentational photography and fab vegan dishes; Barefoot Chef, Dave Richards; Valentine Warner; Mrs Gupta; and where would we be without Rich and his sausage puns? Thanks too to Punkettes Shelley and Amy for being star chefs at Wowo.

Thanks to you!

Finally, and most importantly, a BIG THANK YOU goes to all those who took the time to write down and send in their favourite campsite cuisine recipes. Those who've made Jamie Oliver/Delia Smith status in Punk HQ (one or two of us regularly cook your recipes!) are: Helen (Napom) Gradidge for her Four-Can Stew, Wake-Me-Up Omelette Brekkie and Chunky Hash, Valentine Warner for his Lambs' Liver Kebabs, Sophie Mautner-Hudson for her Stewy Dumpling Delight, Deb Jowett for her Sweet-Chilli Mackerel, Mamma G for her Spaghetti Fish, Maddie Price for her Tip-Top Guacamole, Jill Hudson for her Camperstrone, Claire Guillon for her Moroccan Couscous with Halloumi, Nicki Hatton for her Veggie Chilli, Robert and Kirsty McMurdo for their Camper's Catalan Stew, Natalie Cook for her Superfood Smash, George Chapman for his Smackerel of Mackerel on Garlic Bread and Romany Greatrex for her Tin Cakes.